Additional Praise for
The Commercial Real Estate Tsunami

"Tony Wood has compiled more than just valuable information about commercial real estate; this book shares actionable insights that will inform both commercial real estate professionals as well as their business owner clients. What makes this book standout is that it is more than just a warning of a challenging market, but an invaluable roadmap that offers specific strategies to guide brokers, clients and others through this crisis."
—Doug Frye, President and CEO, CMN, Inc., Colliers International

"The coming wave of loan defaults in commercial real estate deals will create major downward pressures on the general recovery of the U.S. economy. Many borrowers will lose their properties and many lenders will lose money. Those directly engaged in commercial property markets on any level will find many practical suggestions in this book to cope with these dire future events."
—Anthony Downs, Senior Fellow, Metropolitan Policy Department, Brookings Institution, Author, *Real Estate and the Financial Crisis*

"*The Commercial Real Estate Tsunami* should have a lasting place on any commercial real estate professional's bookshelf not just for managing today's investment real estate bust but also for recognizing the signs of the next, inevitable real estate investment boom and to better position yourself and your business to avoid getting caught up in the tides of this cyclical marketplace."
—Michael Gottlieb, Editor, *California Real Estate Journal*

"Tony's book goes beyond a traditional analytical framework by placing elements of the commercial real estate finance crisis under a microscope and pairs market observations with actionable strategies to operate in challenging times. He covers the spectrum from underlying fundamentals through loan triage for lenders to strategies for borrowers to best-practices for brokers . . . all delivered with relevant support from industry experts. A sturdy guide for difficult times."
—Owen Rouse, President, CORFAC International

"Mr. Wood does an excellent job of revealing not only the probable crisis in commercial real estate but most importantly the danger and fallacy of any policy that allows those who overpaid or lent too much to 'extend and pretend.'"
—Christopher N. Macke, Chief Executive Officer, General Equity Real Estate

"... a thorough effort in understanding the current size and scope of the issues facing the CRE Industry, its economic importance in the overall economy, along with some very practical and real world ideas for improving the current situation and surviving the inevitable shock for all interested parties. Opportunity favors the prepared mind and Tony helps clear away the fear by preparing a playbook for the eventual long range investment opportunities that will arise when the Tsunami waters recede. Very nice work!"
—Jim McCarthy, Chief Operating Officer,
Legacy Capital Management, Inc.

"The meltdown of commercial real estate will affect our country for years to come and cost owners and lenders hundreds of billions of dollars in losses. This is a must read for developers, professionals, lenders, brokers, investors and business owners everywhere."
—Michael Hawes, CPA and Principal, Michael Hawes & Associates

"The pending commercial lending debacle will have a tremendous impact on the economy unless we take preemptive measures. Tony Wood is an insightful real estate broker and has encapsulated the issue for the layman to understand."
—Mark Giovanzana, Senior Vice President, Colliers International

"Tony does a fine job of presenting a well documented anthology of the events and causes leading up to *The Commercial Real Estate Tsunami* as well as provides a must read 'Survival Guide' for all of the professions that have a 'seat at the table' of Commercial Investment Real Estate."
—Robert B. Toothaker, CPM, Chairman, CB Richard Ellis Bradley;
National Association of Realtors, 2009 Chair of
The Realtors Commercial Alliance

The Commercial Real Estate Tsunami

Founded in 1807, John Wiley & Sons is the oldest independent publishing company in the United States. With offices in North America, Europe, Australia, and Asia, Wiley is globally committed to developing and marketing print and electronic products and services for our customers' professional and personal knowledge and understanding.

The Wiley Finance series contains books written specifically for finance and investment professionals as well as sophisticated individual investors and their financial advisors. Book topics range from portfolio management to e-commerce, risk management, financial engineering, valuation, and financial instrument analysis, as well as much more.

For a list of available titles, visit our Web site at www.WileyFinance.com.

The Commercial Real Estate Tsunami

A Survival Guide for Lenders, Owners, Buyers, and Brokers

TONY WOOD

Foreword by
Matthew Anderson,
Foresight Analytics

John Wiley & Sons, Inc.

Published by John Wiley & Sons, Inc., Hoboken, New Jersey.

Published simultaneously in Canada.

Market Survey Data Provided by CoStar Group

For general information on our other products and services or for technical support, please contact our Customer Care Department within the United States at (800) 762-2974, outside the United States at (317) 572-3993 or fax (317) 572-4002.

Wiley also publishes its books in a variety of electronic formats. Some content that appears in print may not be available in electronic books. For more information about Wiley products, visit our web site at www.wiley.com.

Library of Congress Cataloging-in-Publication Data:

Wood, Tony.
    The commercial real estate tsunami : a survival guide for lenders, owners, buyers, and brokers / Tony Wood ; foreword by Matthew Anderson.
        p. cm.
    Includes index.
    ISBN 978-0-470-62682-5 (cloth)
        1. Commercial real estate—United States.   2. Commercial loans—United States.
3. Mortgage loans—United States.   I. Title.
    HD1393.58.U6W66 2011
    333.33'870973—dc22

                                                                    2009054064

Printed in the United States of America
10 9 8 7 6 5 4 3 2 1

*To my wife, Donna, and our three children,
Campbell, Aidan, and Aspen:
Waves of joy and inspiration
follow wherever you go,
making life better for those in your wake.*

Contents

Foreword

This Time Is Different

It has been said that the four most dangerous words in the English language are, "This time is different." There are several factors that make this downturn feel different. The most worrisome is the record amount of commercial mortgages coming due—a tsunami of debt—as we head deeper into the commercial real estate downturn. Combined with the weakest economic and financial conditions in generations, this tsunami of debt threatens to derail a nascent economic recovery and hit the financial markets with a second round of losses. This book arrives then as the commercial real estate industry is staggering under the weight of debt amassed during a commercial real estate boom, not unlike the residential real estate boom-and-bust that has laid waste to the national, regional, and local economies. We are still in the earlier phases of this downturn—as Tony points out, the commercial real estate market was essentially running on fumes for most of 2008, and the plunge in prices at the heart of our current problems really only gathered momentum from late-2008 into 2009. And by most accounts, this drop in prices probably has further to go before hitting bottom.

As Tony and the other contributors to this book point out, the real estate market has gone through boom/bust cycles before. So, while the severity of the issue is off the charts, there are definitely many features in common with previous cycles; moreover, there are mechanisms to deal with it—foreclosure and workouts to name a couple—that are clearly described herein.

This book fills a void in our understanding of the causes of the crisis, and more importantly should help market participants—investors, developers, lenders, and brokers—get vitally needed perspective on where we might be going next and how we will get there. The commercial real estate downturn of the 1980s and 1990s and subsequent recovery provides us with hope that frozen markets can be unfrozen, as well as plenty of "lessons learned" that are every bit as applicable now as then.

So read on, and gain insights from some folks who have plenty of lessons for today's market, as well as hard-won perspective gained from having lived through previous cycles.

Matthew Anderson
Partner, Foresight Analytics, LLC
Oakland, California

tsu•na•mi (tsoo-nä -me)
n. pl. -mis, -mi

1. A very large wave caused by an unforeseen event; often results in extreme destruction when it strikes; an event resulting in great loss and misfortune 2. A sudden increase in overwhelming number or volume

sur•vive (ser-viv)
v. sur•vived, sur•viv•ing, sur•vives

1. To remain alive or in existence 2. To carry on despite hardships or trauma; persevere 3. To remain functional or usable 4. To live longer than; outlive 5. To live, persist, or remain usable through 6. To cope with (a trauma or setback); persevere after

Introduction

A Tsunami Warning: Between Fear and Desperation

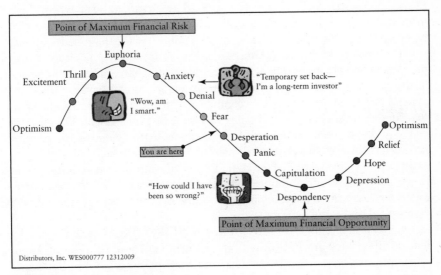

FIGURE I.1 The Cycle of Market Emotions

Source: Westcore Funds distributed by ALPS. Copyright September 1998, Denver Investments, all rights reserved.

It is rapidly becoming a well-known fact throughout the financial markets and commercial real estate industry that a tsunami is imminent for the commercial real estate industry. This tsunami is not comprised of water but of debt. All indications are that the trillion-plus dollars of commercial real estate loan maturities between 2010 through 2013 combined with the commercial real estate markets being battered by the economic collapse we are currently experiencing will result in conditions the marketplace has never seen before. Exactly how much of the estimated $6 trillion value of the nation's commercial real estate will be lost is difficult to know, but the losses will be historic in size and breadth. The impact on banks and other lending institutions nationwide will result in closures not seen since the Savings and Loan (S&L) crisis of the 1980s or The Great Depression. The situation is urgent and requires immediate attention. This is evidenced by the growing political and media discussions of the subject and the commercial real estate institutions that have agreed to be contributors to this book. CCIM Institute; Foresight Analytics; Maura O'Connor, Partner of Seyfarth Shaw LLP and author of the Globe St. blog Practical Counsel; Dr. Sam Chandan, Real Estate Econometrics; Tom Loeswick of Shirlaws, a global business coaching firm; and many others have not only helped make this book an important wake-up call to the industry, but also offer solutions for the journey ahead.

This book is the first of its kind in many ways. It is the first book to address the phenomena of the pending wave of commercial debt maturities coming due in the next five years and the impact those maturities will have on the commercial real estate markets when combined with the historic economic crisis the world is experiencing at this time. This is the first time CoStar Group, with one of the largest commercial real estate databases in the United States, has ever provided its market survey data for a book. Never before has such a group of experts from varied sectors of the commercial real estate industry come together to provide insights and solutions for the anticipated wave of commercial real estate debt maturities, the resulting foreclosures, loss of value, and the battered commercial real estate marketplace.

Commercial real estate foreclosures and REOs (Real Estate Owned by lenders taken back in foreclosures), commercial loan modifications and loan workouts, new investor expectations, and property management challenges combined with the survival of commercial real estate firms across the country will all be major issues to contend with in the months and years ahead. The psychological impact on commercial real estate investors in every market is already reflected in part by the stunning drop in sales activity (Figure I.1). These concerns are addressed in this book with solutions anyone in the commercial real estate industry can benefit from. In my 34 years in the commercial real estate industry I have seen many kinds of markets, properties, and ownership trends. I have represented most every kind of owner of commercial real estate, from Fortune 500 companies to local 7-Eleven stores, well-known retailers and huge distribution facilities, apartments, shopping centers, and industrial buildings. My work throughout the western United States has included consulting to major banks and insurance companies as my clients in the disposition of their properties that had been taken back in foreclosure. I survived the 1980s, years of double-digit inflation, high double-digit interest rates, and soaring unemployment. Then the savings and loan crisis of the late 1980s arrived, bringing us the Resolution Trust Corporation (the RTC) and liquidation of commercial real estate valued in the billions selling for pennies on the dollar throughout the early 1990s. In Silicon Valley we witnessed firsthand the dotcom boom and bust. We now see what could possibly be the worst catastrophe the U.S. commercial real estate industry has ever experienced approaching. A historic wave of commercial real estate foreclosures is imminent, combined with an economic collapse not seen since the great depression.

Tsunami may seem like a rather dramatic term to use certainly for the title of my book; however, the more I researched the situation, the more I realized that what we are about to experience has many similarities to a tsunami, at least in terms of an analogy. A tsunami is an event that is typically unseen and unexpected until it's too late; it then hits with such ferocity anyone caught in its path has little chance of survival.

It is my intention that this book not only send out a "tsunami warning" to the commercial real estate industry but that it also offer concrete solutions and ways to mitigate the risks and hazards that lie ahead of us. Commercial lending institutions, owners and landlords of commercial real estate, buyers, tenants, and commercial real estate brokers can all benefit by preparing now. Some of the solutions and ideas submitted in this book are very simple common sense recommendations that will be easy to act on now; others will literally take an act of Congress to implement. One of the most surprising discoveries I made while doing research for this book is that there were many people writing about the problem but very few submitting any tangible solutions to the challenge.

As you read this book you will hear from recognized experts in the commercial real estate industry and financial markets. These knowledgeable, experienced, and balanced individuals and organizations provide useful ideas and guidance we can all benefit from. You will see more clearly than ever before what is happening in the commercial real estate marketplace and the commercial lending markets. You will discover the need for action now. Professionally, you will learn of actions you can take that will protect you and your company. This book also presents ideas and opportunities to actively support those organizations fighting to make the changes needed to thwart the hazards that our marketplace and very livelihoods face.

It is also my intention for this book to help raise the level of alert and bring all sectors of commercial real estate and members of Congress to the table, providing solutions resulting in an outcome better than what lies ahead if we do nothing at all.

Acknowledgments

I want to thank my wife, Donna Wood, who is a writer and family therapist, and whose expert guidance and support was crucial to the writing and publishing of this book. This book was first conceived in a conversation between Donna and me as we discussed the national wave of commercial real estate debt I saw headed our way and the disastrous impact it would have on the entire commercial real estate industry. Her encouragement that day (and in the days and months that followed) inspired me to write this book and to create something that would contribute to the solution. In the end she too would add her written contribution to the book supporting the human element impacted by the commercial real estate tsunami.

There are several people and organizations I must acknowledge personally, for without them this book would not have been possible: Edward M. Bury, APR, and the CCIM Institute; Brandon King and Tim Trainor at CoStar Group. Matthew Anderson at Foresight Analytics was the first to agree to be a contributor and then later to write my Foreword. My friend and partner at TRI Commercial Real Estate Services, Gordon Stevenson, and his wife Dr. Mary G. Johnson, both of whom supported me in obtaining the resources I needed. TRI Commercial Real Estate Services, CORFAC International, for its support throughout my many years of association with them, particularly our staff, Cindy Murphy, Nancy Huggett, and Mike Murphy. Bart Campbell, whose commitment and masterful technical support was invaluable to me.

Contributors: From CCIM Institute, Charles A. "Mac" McClure and Cynthia Shelton; Eric Von Berg, Newmark Realty Capital; Maura O'Connor, Seyfarth Shaw LLP; Dr. Sam Chandan, Real Estate Econometrics; Tom Loeswick of Shirlaws Business Coaching; and Anton Qiu of TRI Commercial have all generously shared their knowledge and expertise in this book.

Finally, John Wiley & Sons and my editor, Laura Walsh, for the courage and vision to take my manuscript and put it on the fast track to be one of the first books in the world published on this subject.

It's been a long road travelled in record time. Thank you all for your service and commitment to this work.

Tony Wood

Phases of the Tsunami

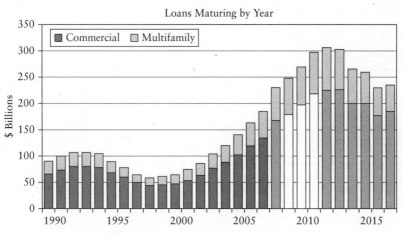

Loans Maturing by Year

Commercial and Multifamily Mortgage Maturities

Source: Copyright 2009 Foresight Analytics, LLC

Phase One: Initiation (2005–2007)

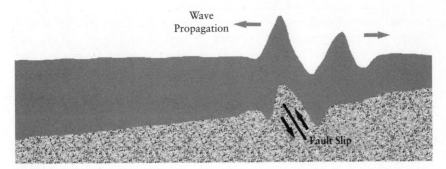

FIGURE 1.1 Initiation Phase

OBSERVING A WAVE OF CRISIS

Tsunamis have several stages, the first of which is called Initiation. As shown in Figure 1.1, Initiation is when something occurs that is typically unseen and unheard but that generates the conditions for a tsunami to occur. Initiation for the commercial real estate tsunami wave headed our way was caused in part by the same kind of exuberance in the marketplace that led to the residential housing market collapse. Ownership fever spread widely, driven by economic, political, and social pressures and facilitated by enthusiastic lenders with an optimistic posture that matched the marketplace.

Wall Street then offered expanded opportunities to securitize and otherwise participate in the profit of this trend and many of the loans facilitating it. These actions echoed many of the conditions and causes that have led us to the residential real estate fiasco we are still recovering from today. The booming economy of the mid 2000s pushed commercial rents up, and high valuation followed. Adding to the momentum was the availability of financing for commercial properties, fueled in part by commercial mortgage backed securities (CMBS). The collapse of our economy late in 2008, and the resulting fall of commercial real estate values, has left us with over $1 trillion in commercial real estate loans maturing in the next few years, and great challenges to refinance them. When did we start talking so casually in trillions of dollars like they are estimates to get our home remodeled? That answer you will find in the Amplification phase, discussed in Chapter 2.

Commercial financing through CMBS is similar in structure to the securitized residential mortgages known as mortgage-backed securities (MBS). Through the mid 2000s, as demand for commercial real estate increased, so did the need to finance it. CMBS helped fuel the availability of financing for commercial real estate throughout the nation and became part of the "Initiation" of the wave we see before us today. Despite the fact that most experts believe lending practices remained relatively conservative throughout the boom, no one could have predicted the free fall in occupancy, rental rates, and values we see today and expect in the months and years ahead. In 2009 new origination of CMBS was nowhere to be seen and seems unlikely to return to previous levels any time in the near future. Where CMBS left off, banks, large and small, all across the country took over, ultimately making loans that would later cost many of these institutions their economic lives.

It would appear commercial real estate markets are about two years behind the residential markets. In the coming years we will see a very familiar pattern of deteriorating values and industry and government intervention with a long recovery ahead. Unfortunately, during the height of the boom throughout 2005, 2006, and 2007, the underwriters of these loans continued to be very optimistic about commercial property's stability and did not anticipate the perfect storm headed our way.

On March 26, 2009 the *Wall Street Journal* ran a front-page article titled "Commercial Property Faces Crisis." In this article, the Journal reported, "The delinquency rate on about 700 billion securitized (CMBS) loans backed by office buildings and hotels and stores and other investment property has more than doubled since September." These delinquency rates have continued to rise at an unprecedented rate. This is very similar to the conditions that resulted from the savings and loan crisis and creation of the Resolution Trust Corporation (the RTC) of the late 1980s and early 1990s. The savings and loan crisis resulted in the failure of close to a thousand U.S. banks and savings institutions. To put things in perspective, however, the lenders at the time only took about $48 billion in losses on commercial real estate debt between 1990 and 1995, representing about 8 percent of the overall debt. The U.S. banking sector could suffer ten times those losses this time, with the possibility of more than 700 banks failing as a result of the commercial real estate foreclosures that lie ahead. Consider the momentum of devaluation potentially impacting the overall commercial real estate market. That's just the beginning. Of the $500 billion in commercial loans held by smaller community banks, a large percentage could not be refinanced if they were due today, and that's just what will be maturing between 2010 and 2013!

Estimates are that about two-thirds of the estimated $700 billion in CMBS maturities won't qualify for refinancing. The *Wall Street Journal* article also stated, "Besides securities backed by commercial real estate loans about $524.5 billion of the whole commercial mortgages held by the nation's bank and thrifts are expected to come due between this year and 2012. Between 40% and 45% of those loans wouldn't qualify for refinancing in the tight credit environment as they exceed 90% of the underlying properties' values, estimates Matthew Andersen, partner at Foresight Analytics."

The Foresight Analytics report that much of the *Wall Street Journal* article was based on is called "Commercial Mortgage Outlook: Growing Pains in Mortgage Maturities" and is an excellent source of data on this subject. Dated March 17, 2009, the report states: "The commercial real estate market faces demand for mortgage financing, at a time when credit is very tight. This is setting the stage for a likely financing shortfall, leading to increased distress in the commercial real estate debt market and putting further downward pressure on values." Adding, "Foresight Analytics estimates that $814 billion in commercial and multifamily mortgages will mature between 2009 to 2011 (see the figure on page 1). Commercial mortgages, at $594 billion, will comprise the bulk of the maturities. . . ." Some commercial property values have already fallen more than 50 percent form their inflated 2007 values, exceeding losses resulting from the S&L crisis of the 1990s.

McClatchy Washington Bureau posted April 29, 2009, ". . .'it's the next big wave to hit. It's the next round of bad news,' said Scott Talbot, the senior vice president of government affairs for the Financial Services Roundtable, a trade group for big banks and other financial institutions collectively concerned about the coming problems."

On April 16, 2009, General Growth properties filed for bankruptcy protection. The Chicago-based company owned more than 200 malls across the United States at the time. General Growth was unable to renegotiate its debts as they came due at the time of the filing.

Paul Walter, vice president of brokerage operations in North America for NAI Global, was quoted as saying, "On the street, the rumor is it is coming and it's going to come fast and furious." Moreover, Christopher Cornell, commercial real estate economist for Moody's Economy.com asserts, "There will be a further drag on the economy's recovery." These foreboding warnings keep coming everyday, with no end in sight.

The bad news continued to build throughout 2009: Finally, there was news that President Obama was being introduced to the issue in October when Fox Business News published in an exclusive on Friday, October 16, 2009: "FBN Exclusive: Obama Briefed on Commercial Real Estate." The article, by Peter Barnes of Fox Business with the subtitle "Commercial Real Estate: The Next Crisis," went on to say, "President Obama was formally briefed by his economic team recently on growing problems in commercial real estate lending, an administration official told Fox Business. According to the administration official, the economic team briefed the President on the 'looming issue,' an issue many believe could trigger the next banking crisis."

Intelligent Investing published "Commercial Real Estate Will Collapse" by Stuart Saft on November 19, 2009, which stated, "The long-feared financial disaster is still looming. Bad court decisions could set it off. The commercial real estate market is on its last legs and unless drastic actions are taken, the effects on the broader economy will be catastrophic. The obvious problem is the excessive amount of debt placed on the properties and the amount of debt that has to be refinanced during a relatively short period of time." Then this from Bloomberg.com on December 7, 2009, "No Escape from TARP for U.S. Banks Choking on Real Estate Loans," by Elizabeth Hester and Linda Shen. "As the U.S. economy pulls out of a recession and the biggest banks return to profitability, mounting defaults on commercial property may keep regional lenders from repaying bailout funds until at least 2011. Unpaid loans on malls, hotels, apartments and home developments stood at a 16-year high of 3.4 percent in the third quarter of 2009 and are continuing to rise at an alarming rate. Nationwide, the volume of estimated commercial and multifamily mortgage maturities is also a serious concern as shown in Table 1.1.

UNDER WATER AND SINKING FAST

Here lies one of the fundamental challenges to the commercial loan maturity issue; while it is estimated that the total debt on commercial real estate nationwide is $3.5 trillion on an estimated $6 trillion of value, the estimated loan-to-value ratio on the majority of loans maturing between 2010 and 2013 was on average 70 to 80 percent. Keep in mind that the 70 to 80 percent loan to value ratio was established at the time these loans were originated, during the boom. Given the overall reduction in commercial real estate values, most of these loans could not be refinanced without a

TABLE 1.1 Estimated Mortgage Maturities, 2009 to 2011 in Bank and Thrift Portfolios, Commercial and Multifamily Mortgages (in $billions)

	2009 to 2011 Maturities		
State	**$ Amount**	**State**	**$ Amount**
California	$44.3	Maryland	$4.3
New York	$31.0	Mississippi	$4.2
Illinois	$24.3	Kansas	$4.1
Florida	$21.0	Iowa	$4.0
Texas	$20.3	Connecticut	$3.9
Georgia	$15.9	Utah	$3.9
Wisconsin	$15.3	Arizona	$3.7
Pennsylvania	$12.7	Nevada	$3.7
Missouri	$12.1	Nebraska	$2.7
Michigan	$11.5	Oregon	$2.7
New Jersey	$11.0	New Mexico	$1.8
North Carolina	$ 8.8	West Virginia	$1.7
Minnesota	$ 8.2	Maine	$1.6
Ohio	$ 8.0	New Hampshire	$1.6
Tennessee	$ 7.6	Delaware	$1.4
Massachusetts	$ 7.5	Montana	$1.3
Louisiana	$ 6.4	South Dakota	$1.2
Virginia	$ 6.4	Idaho	$1.1
Arkansas	$ 6.1	North Dakota	$1.1
Washington	$ 6.0	District of Columbia	$0.8
Alabama	$ 5.8	Vermont	$0.8
Colorado	$ 5.7	Wyoming	$0.7
Oklahoma	$ 5.5	Rhode Island	$0.6
Indiana	$ 5.1	Hawaii	$0.5
Kentucky	$ 5.0	Alaska	$0.4
South Carolina	$ 5.0		

Source: Foresight Analytics, LLC, 2009

considerable principal reduction by the borrower or other kind of loan workout with the lender. How many owners will opt to make principal reductions on their failing commercial real estate investments is one question; how many will have the financial ability to do it if they wish to is another.

Original loan-to-value ratios on many of the $500 billion commercial loans also maturing between 2010 and 2013 with the smaller community banks could easily exceed the value of the property itself. Many of these loans were made to small businesses that are currently struggling with the economic conditions and are likely to fall into default in the coming months and years ahead.

Estimates of the total value of the nation's commercial real estate range between $6 and $7 trillion. This value was driven to this level by the huge demand of the boom economy to house its businesses and workplaces. Office buildings, shopping centers, industrial buildings, and manufacturing plants are the homes of the businesses that drive our economy. Drugstores, bicycle shops, hair salons, auto repair shops, and grocery stores are places we visit daily and depend on. As the economy declines and the demand for services and products decreases, so does the demand for commercial real estate.

During the last five years of our booming economy, we couldn't construct buildings fast enough; multiple offers to purchase or lease buildings were commonplace nationwide. If it sounds familiar, it's because it echoes the residential real estate boom we were experiencing at the same time. Commercial real estate demand is directly correlated to growth in areas like construction, housing, and consumer affluence. Using their homes as virtual ATMs, many consumers spent more than they otherwise could have (or should have), and demand for all things retail increased exponentially. On and on it went until late last year when the startling press conferences from Washington and New York announced our economy was on the verge of collapse. No one had noticed?!. The fall came with virtually no warning whatsoever.

It was a downward (or upward depending on how you look at it) spiral: Consumers over-leveraged their homes, using them as ATMs for their spending sprees. Over a period of years this activity led to overinflated sales projections, which in turn led to overinflated expectations for continued consumer demand and inaccurate projections for the demand for all types of commercial real estate—retail, office, and industrial.

A VIEW FROM HIGHER GROUND—CHARLES A. "MAC" MCCLURE, 2009 PRESIDENT CCIM INSTITUTE

A Certified Commercial Investment Member (CCIM) is one of the most recognized expert certifications in the commercial real estate industry. CCIM Institute is the world's largest network for commercial real estate professionals. When I sat down with Charles A. "Mac" McClure, 2009 president of CCIM Institute and prolific commercial real estate broker, I knew this was going to be a great opportunity for readers to learn a few things about what our industry is going through and benefit from the depth of Mac's knowledge and experience. Along with being the 2009 president of CCIM Institute, Mac is Chairman of the Board of McClure Partners, a full-service real estate brokerage and development company based in Addison, Texas, part of the Dallas-Fort Worth metroplex. Mac entered the real estate profession in 1975 and was President and co-founder of TIG Real Estate Services, Inc., of Dallas, a real estate holding company set up to manage, lease, and develop real estate for pension funds, REITs, and insurance companies.

During his 34-year real estate career, Mr. McClure has closed more than $1 billion of real estate transactions and negotiated over $500 million in lease transactions. Mac is a licensed real estate broker in the state of Texas and holds both the prestigious CCIM and CRE designations. Mr. McClure has authored numerous articles on commercial real estate, is a nationally known speaker on the subject, and has managed, leased, and developed for and consulted with many of the largest pension funds and institutional investors in the United States.

The CCIM trait runs in his family as he is married to Susan McClure, CCIM, and has one son John McClure, CCIM, who are partners with him in his firm. Mac was gracious enough to grant me the following interview.

Tony Wood: Mac, you and I have been in the business over 30 years; we have both seen some very severe markets. One of the worst was working through the S&L crisis of the 1980s and the RTC program. I remember in reading about your history that you had some involvement with the commercial real estate industry's recovery yourself during that time?
Charles A. "Mac" McClure: Yes, I was. I had originally written the troubled assets course for the CCIM Institute in 1986, and in 1986, 1987, and 1988 we called it the "REO Super Session" in Dallas, Texas, and that's all we were doing back in those days.

TW: I would imagine you are planning on bringing something similar back to the CCIM curriculum these days.
CM: We have talked about that. One problem is it is almost impossible to get your hands around what we are dealing with today. And, quite candidly, I have spent more time probably lobbying than I have worrying about that, because I represent some of the major pension funds in America. For the last fifteen years this list has included CALPers, New York State Teachers, GE Capital, various police and fire associations, State of Alaska Permanent Fund, and one of the things that I have found is the real problem today is mark to market accounting rules. In 2007 FASB passed the famous "157 rule," which created more problems and the

biggest tsunami that has happened in the commercial real estate—really in the world economy—since the Great Depression. It was a non-governmental agency that created the problem under the osmosis of the Securities and Exchange Commission.

TW: Can you give us some detail on the FASB (Financial Accounting Standards Board) 157 rule?

CM: FASB 157 in 2007 changed the evaluation technique for any mortgage or investment vehicle for the residential and commercial real estate markets. FASB 157 set the standards that said that you had to use only one approach to value under FASB's "fair accounting value." Or, stated differently, an auditor who audits a pool of loans securing CMBS bonds for a pension fund, insurance company, or bank will evaluate with only one approach to value, which is the sales comparison approach—in FASB words, "Active Trading Market." When you have no active trading market for the bonds, then the value will be written down to the level of those bonds that are trading. The accountant becomes the appraiser of the bonds under FASB 157 and has to use one of three tests: level one is active trading market, level two observable market data, or level three (with auditors' discretion) discounted cash flow. However, accountants are not used to using three approaches to value like appraisers in the real estate industry, and when an FASB ruling comes out, they will go to the first one and use it since they feel that this is the most defensible approach.

So, in essence, instead of using the true three approaches to value that real estate appraisers use under FIRREA, FASB has basically told the appraisers of the loans to use only one approach to value, which has really messed the entire market up. We have the building being appraised with three approaches and the underlying loan with one approach—does that make sense? Hell, no.

TW: So the appraisal of the loan has no correlation with the real estate. As you said, real estate appraisers use the standard three approaches of comparable sales, replacement cost, and income approach, right?

CM: That's right, so you have current sales of similar buildings, which is the comparable sales approach, you have cost approach, and you have income approach. The regulators ordered the MAI appraisers, "You will use them, all of them." When my office building is being appraised under those three approaches today by the real estate appraisers, but the underlying mortgage is being appraised by another entirely different approach to value by the accountants, then we have a disconnect from the marketplace. So the appraisal for the underlying loan says you will use the sales comparable approach and maybe you can use some observable market data, and maybe you can use some discounted cash flow, but you really need to use active trading market. Well, there was no active trading market in 2008, and by the time the auditors finished all of their rewriting of the books, every bank, every pension fund, and every insurance company in America was undercapitalized because the auditors went in and took a non-trading market and wrote down their pools of mortgages as much as 40, 50, or 60 percent of the value the year before.

So let me give you a really good example: A medium-sized police and fire association has $50 million in Triple A rated CMBS offerings, now they are at the bottom tranche of the CMBS portfolio. There's no active trading market, so the auditor sits there and says, "Well, we can't find any comparables. The only comps we have are these deeply discounted loans that are selling, so that must be the comparable. Thus, we are going to write your pool of loans down from $50 million to $22 million. Even though it is still cash flowing, even though you're still getting the same $3.5 million in return, and even though you have a net operating income of three and a half million dollars, we are going to write it down to $22 million." This means that the police and fire association will now have to reserve for $30 million in losses. As a pension fund, the guy that made the investment gets to go to the firehouse and sit there and get the crap beat out of him because he quote "lost $30 million" when he really didn't.

TW: Give me your estimation as to what the reserve requirement looks like on something like that.

CM: Just go look at loan loss reserve requirements, if you take $30 million off somebody's balance sheet. Let's talk about what a pension fund has to do. A bank has 10 percent capital; if it's a billion-dollar bank, that means it has to have $100 million in capital to keep that 10 percent capital ratio. Let's say a pension fund has to have $100 million at 10 percent or $10 million. So if it's a billion dollars, you have to have 10 percent or $100 million.

Then all of a sudden you lose $30 million of equity on a portfolio of triple A bonds, but you were still getting the same cash flow. That means your capitalization went from a $100 million to $70 million immediately on a billion dollar fund. That's exactly what happened—that is exactly what is happening everywhere.

If you're a $500 million pension fund, take 10 percent of that, $50 million, right? And if you took $30 million out of the $50 million does that screw up all of your ratios? Dramatically? Immediately? Now you are running around scrambling—trying to figure out how you're going to do it, you might even have to go sell that pool.

TW: Mac, I am sure that you know as well as anyone, that while the auditors are a pain in their approach, there is some credence to the concept that we have some loss of value to deal with, isn't there?

CM: Yes, we have loss of value. We overextended ourselves. We had a rather large segment of the population do what? They went out and got sub-prime mortgages, and there are some people in the country who shouldn't have homeownership, period.

TW: I am sure you have seen the numbers already, this trillion-dollar wave of commercial debt maturities over the next several years, and the whole mark to market concerns that you're addressing here. I look at it from a more fundamental standpoint because I'm not a mortgage banker, I'm a commercial real estate broker. These days I'm selling mostly commercial REOs and commercial short sales at deeply discounted prices from what their "market value" was estimated at just a year or two ago. It is very difficult to find a "market value price" because there isn't a market anymore to get a pulse on. You said earlier, it's hard to get your arms around the problem. It seems we're in a free fall. Vacancy rates are skyrocketing, rental rates are plummeting, that automatically equates to reduction in values, cap rates have increased—there's some more reduction in value, and then you've got this limitation on financing that's going to strangle our ability to do transactions. These equate to real actual adjustments in value as well—don't they?
CM: Yes, and here's something else: My biggest problem is I'm taking these issues to Congress and I can't get anyone to listen. Nobody wants to have a congressional hearing about it, but that's where we are.

TW: But even if these rules did not exist, wouldn't we still be looking at these vacancy rates and rental rates and looking at some significant decreases in value?
CM: First, I will say that California, Arizona, and Florida are kicked out of the equation—and the only reason that I say that is because I have seen—and I don't mean this unkindly—I've seen a tremendous amount of speculation going on in those three markets in all product types, including residential.

Where it's a little different is most of the rest of the country. You see a slow down, and when you see a slow down and you go into a recession, you start seeing consumer confidence waning. All that shrinks the market. Therefore, you have tenants like Circuit City going out of business, you have people in the market who are overcapitalized and having problems, but that is probably only 15 to 20 percent with problems—not 60 percent problems. And I guess that is where my problem with the whole thing is.

If you look across the board, the real estate value cycle should have been somewhere around an 18 to 20 percent correction. That means if you had a $5 million building, then you should be looking at something like a million dollar correction off that building's value, where now it is worth $4 million.

But because there's no accounting, because there is no way to finance the building. It's going down even more and the mortgage underneath it has been traded at $2 million instead of $4 million.

The entire market is being run based on a panic mode instead of a real economic mode. Now you are going to see this trillion dollars (coming due). The thing that's interesting is if we are dealing with borrowers with triple A underlying assets, generally speaking, they are going to figure out a way to renew those notes, but if you're dealing with someone like a Dollar General deal with a "mom and pop" owner or a "mom and pop" barber shop, then that's not going to work; they are the ones who are going to have a grave problem.

TW: That is what I am really concerned about. The large pension funds and REITs will find a way or die, but it's going to be the smaller investors out there, many of the people I deal with everyday, that are really going to be impacted. The $1, $3, $5, $8 million properties. The owner-users and single-tenant, triple net leased investments, they are not going to fare well under these market conditions. Many of the small investors and small partnerships are now upside down, owing more than the property is worth. Many of these people tried to do everything right, they put 40 to 50 percent down, but unfortunately when it comes time to renew these loans, they are going to have challenges with that.

Today we've got this trillion dollars of debt coming due, and it was originated at 70 percent loan to value. You and I both know that even on your most conservative estimates, whereby you eliminated my favorite states of California, Arizona, and Florida, we're still looking at situations where they can not renew or refinance those loans. Even if those properties are fully occupied (which a lot of them are not) because their loan to value won't match up. They are going to have to make capital contributions, get a loan workout, or give the property back to the bank.

CM: Ninety-nine percent of the lenders and major pension funds in this country that made the participating loans in the triple A rated type office buildings are going to be okay. Those are the guys that go out and do $150 or $200 million loans, and they will be okay.

The problem I see is these $5 and $10 million deals. If you wipe out the liquidity of a $250 to $500 million bank down Main Street anywhere USA, it can't make a real estate loan because its ratios are so dad-gum upside down.

You have a certain percentage of your portfolio, or you're too heavy in real estate, or you've got too many loan loss reserves set up for the real estate because your portfolio was written down. I know of a bank that bought some really good triple A performing mortgage-backed security pools, and they're sucking eggs right now on their capitalization. They can't make a loan in any real estate assets at all until their ratios come back.

TW: So are you there side by side with Real Estate Roundtable and its five-point plan, or do you have your own lobbying position, and or do you guys work together?
CM: We're there with Real Estate Roundtable, we're there with CMBS (Commercial Mortgage Backed Securities Association), National Association of Realtors, Institute of Real Estate Management, all of us are in there slugging it out together.

TW: Good. The commercial real estate industry needs all the help it can get these days, and we don't exactly have the same political sympathetic ear that homeowners had in the residential sector crisis.
CM: The trouble is that the Congress of the United States spent the entire summer and fall 2009 talking about healthcare, while the rest of the world falls down on top of its head—oh yeah, we're going to get to this next year, if we have a next year.

The future, for the next two to three years, until we see a recovery, all we see is catastrophic things, or until we see some reason that we're going to jump out of it. From 1930 to 1940 the unemployment rate continued to be the same. In fact, for all of the New Deal efforts that FDR put in, every one of them, the unemployment rate still went up by the time they got through with all the job growth and all they were shoving down our throats. By 1939 our unemployment rate was higher than it was in 1930 and 1931. Eventually, we will figure out that shoving money out of the government trough doesn't work, and then we're going to have to have job growth. When we start having job growth, then this country will start coming around again—but you know we're at a very high unemployment rate, so what are we going to do? You and I and every other CCIM in the country are going to sit there and do one thing, we're going to be paddling water and working this out.

We have got to have job growth, real jobs, because real jobs create 3.4 percent more jobs. Then the retail sector and everything else will improve and people can start spending money again.

TW: CCIM Institute curriculum, is that going to change here in the next year? I would imagine it has to.
CM: We have dramatically changed our core courses. We just spent a tremendous amount of money and have rewritten the CCIM 101, 102, 103, and 104 core courses. We are actually using a technique in our 101 that transitions all the way through our courses now. You have two basic kinds of property that you deal with in this country, you have owner-user property and you have investment property. That's it.

So what we have done now with our core courses is incorpeate the concept of Geospatial, GIS, and Cycle Graphics. The commercial real estate space industry is finite, we know what's available. What we need to do is begin to look at the demand side of it. What we have finally started doing is taking the available space versus how we can project demand, which creates the market vacancy for the area. Then we can start pulling it back with Geospatial graphing and Cycle Graphics and determine how to pull that vacancy back into equilibrium.

Our new four courses of the CCIM program have been rewritten because we want to be on the cutting edge. We just spent $2.6 million rewriting them, and it just so happens we're rolling all those courses out and training our instructors in throughout 2010.

TW: Are you going to have any specialty courses on commercial REOs, on lender-client-type relations, on lease or loan renegotiations?

CM: Yes, but to be honest with you, we're taking a more proactive approach with our core courses. Our core courses really and truly are going to dig into the, so to speak, bowels of the entire model. The supply side is pretty much finite retail, office, or industrial. Everything is out there, but what we need to find is new horizons and new corridors for demand, which is going to drive the refilling and re-tenanting of America. To be honest with you, we're real excited about what we're rolling out for 2010.

Number one, we're fixing to revolutionize the industry in my opinion and we're seeing a paradigm shift in the brokerage industry anyway.

TW: Yes—and a paradigm shift by definition means that we can't drive the car using the rearview mirror anymore. We have to start looking ahead and figuring this out ourselves and get ahead of it.

CM: You know we've got 18,000 members, and quite candidly, I am really looking at the possibility of 2010, 2011 repositioning of our membership. CCIM membership will be repositioned and become *the* leading commercial real estate people in the United States. I see the old 50-50 brokerage model as being really top heavy, with that corporate real estate executive sitting in New York or Washington, DC, or wherever the hell they are and taking half of the [broker's fees] and the brokers out there busting their butts. I think you are going to see quite a few of these newer companies, where the broker is actually out there getting 90 percent of the revenue base, because if the tools are available to you through people like the CCIM Institute, what the hell do you need to pay half your income to somebody else for?

TW: Mac, one last question: Would you agree that in the next couple of years as this wave hits that we are going to see lenders as a new and larger client base, and that lenders are going to need to be trained as owners?

CM: Yes—In fact we've had some serious discussions with some of the major lending associations about trying to get them into CCIM 101 to 104 courses. In fact, I'd probably be willing to bet that you're going to see most of the small to medium size banks in America start taking the CCIM courses.

TW: Yes or hiring CCIMs to do some of this REO work for them.
CM: Yes, but you'd have to work for them on a full-time basis.

CHAPTER 2

Phase Two: Amplification (2007–2008)

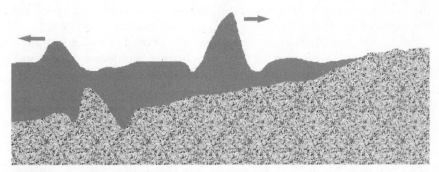

FIGURE 2.1 Amplification Phase

The next stages of a tsunami are called Amplification, Drawdown, and finally the Runup. Amplification, as shown in Figure 2.1, occurs as the tidal wave approaches the shore, causing a phenomenon called Drawdown, just prior to the wave actually running up onto shore. Many of you may remember the devastating tsunami of 2004 and the stories of water ebbing as far back as a mile from the beaches, receding so quickly that fish were left flopping in the wet sand. This was the Drawdown. People were mystified by this strange occurrence just prior to the deluge that followed.

SETTING THE STAGE FOR DRAWDOWN

For the commercial real estate marketplace, it seems the Drawdown of the coming Amplification started in 2009. While some in the commercial real estate industry remained optimistic, taking the stand, "it's just a phase," it's evident in most major metro areas across the nation today that very little is left of an active commercial real estate market.

As we entered 2008 all the necessary elements to initiate the commercial real estate tsunami had been generated.

While it traveled quietly unseen as it approached, it was only a question of when the wave would hit. The Amplification of this wave began in 2008. With the residential real estate sector in the midst of its collapse, funding for commercial real estate loans continued at a brisk pace, unfettered by the economic realities surrounding the marketplace. But the approaching wave began its Amplification as the commercial real estate markets began to feel the influence of the faltering economy and the negative impact the international markets were seeing with the failures of the mortgage-backed securities related to the residential sub-prime loan failures.

As 2008 neared its end, the residential real estate market continued its decline, but the commercial real estate market kept going. Like a huge ship whose engines ran out of fuel yet its own momentum kept surging it forward, the commercial real estate market showed few signs of distress. When the announcements came out last September about the economy (that's when we started talking casually in trillions of dollars!), few in the commercial real estate industry realized the extent of the message and what this meant for the future. But in mid 2009 our "ship" stalled at sea in a dead calm, desperate for the fuel necessary to move forward again.

In commercial real estate, like so many other sectors of the economy, availability of financing combined with a recovering economy and a return of consumer confidence is the fuel we need.

One thing about the history of real estate boom and bust patterns is that it is always difficult to predict exactly when something will happen, but it's obvious when you're there. You don't have to look far to see the 2009 predictions that it is going to get worse before it gets better. Projections of a national vacancy factor of 20 percent in the office sector by the end of 2010 are the highest since 1992. The national effects of these deteriorating conditions are further exemplified in the following chapter with the CoStar Group survey results for the major metro markets throughout the United States.

Any buyer or tenant who is courageous enough to enter the marketplace today, tempted by the low prices, will be doing so in the face of mostly bad news in the media and warnings from friends, family, and coworkers to tread slowly and cautiously if at all. Then those few who brave the low consumer confidence levels will have to successfully survive the erratic, "Da Vinci Code"–like obstacle course that is the process of obtaining a loan on commercial real estate today.

BELOW THE SURFACE

The dramatic decline in demand for space of any kind and the matching reduction in rental rates have pushed values even further down by way of reduced income and higher vacancy rates. These market conditions have increased investor demands for higher returns to match the increased risk, adding additional downward pressure on values.

As more and more businesses fail, tenants are moving out of their spaces at an unprecedented pace across the country. Many tenants are abandoning their space with no notice to the landlord whatsoever, while others have the financial stamina to wait until their lease expires before they downsize to smaller spaces. These factors reinforce increasing vacancy rates, lower values, and even harder to finance properties. The CoStar Group survey results found in Chapter 3 confirm these findings across the board nationally. As these factors have taken root, they have begun to impact the stability of the overall market values of the commercial real estate. And so the Drawdown began.

With the exception of the vulture funds seeking out the few available "distress" opportunities in commercial real estate offered by short sales, foreclosed property auctions, and the purchases of notes on "toxic" assets worthy of their 10 to 30 cent-on-the-dollar offers, there are few "market value" buyers to be seen. The availability of capital for commercial lending is the fuel that makes the engine run, and without it you can't get very far at all. Cash is king! How limiting is that?

When you combine the trillion-plus dollars in loan maturities with a lack of available financing in the worst economy since the Great Depression with tenants and market value buyers few and far between, you have commercial real estate's version of a tsunami's Drawdown effect.

The commercial real estate sector is likely to follow a familiar pattern. Just as the residential market decline started with sub-prime loan failures and aggressive liberal lending standards—conditions that gradually eroded away at the overall market values—commercial owners will likely be damaged with the same "guilt by association."

This is a national dilemma. It's not just the major metro markets that are being affected. Popular, world-famous resort communities such as Mammoth Lakes, one of California's premier ski resorts, have been hit hard. Patty Schwartzkopf, a 30-year real estate veteran at Coldwell Banker-Mammoth Real Estate, reports, "Our stats are very unique. Our sales volume dropped BY 75 percent in 2007; yet, we are bouncing back faster than other markets. Resorts have historically been the last to come back during past declines. Values dropped 45 to 55 percent off their peak at Mammoth. During 2007

and 2008, we had a two-year supply of unsold condos and a 36-month supply of unsold single-family homes. Vacation rentals were down in winter
of 2008–2009. Surprisingly, distressed sales have not exceeded 15 percent of
our business. There is some concern that the next 'wave' of foreclosures
is coming in 2010 and the predicted increase in interest rates could stall the
Mammoth resort market recovery."

Many homeowners who were perfectly good borrowers with excellent
credit, making their payments on time as agreed, can neither sell their homes
for what they owe on them nor refinance them. Receding waters strand
all ships.

Without coordinated intervention and cooperation between property
owners, lenders, commercial real estate industry organizations, and government institutions, we could see a devastating impact on all commercial
real estate values across the board with very few exceptions. Mid 2009 had
many in the commercial real estate industry metaphorically standing on the
beach wondering why the fish were flopping on the wet sand.

LEARNING TO STAY AFLOAT—CYNTHIA SHELTON, 2009 PRESIDENT OF THE FLORIDA ASSOCIATION OF REALTORS

When I began my search for a Florida broker to get some perspective from
that area of the United States, the CCIM Institute referred me to Cynthia
Shelton, CCIM, CRE. Cynthia is the Director of Investment Sales at Colliers
Arnold and 2009 President of the Florida Association of Realtors (FAR).
With over 33 years experience in the real estate industry, Cynthia is responsible for investment sales, primarily retail and office throughout Florida,
providing acquisition and disposition services to private and institutional
clients.

During the past three years as a broker with Colliers Arnold, Cynthia
has contributed to the closing of over 22 investment sale transactions totaling over $85 million in value. Prior to joining the Colliers Arnold team,
Cynthia worked as V.P. of Acquisitions for Commercial Net Lease Realty (a
NYSE-REIT) for 10 years and was responsible for acquisitions of over $300
million in single tenant properties.

This experience gives her a solid insight into the real estate industry as a
whole and the struggles to stay afloat during this difficult time.

Tony Wood: Cynthia, you have an extensive history within the commercial
real estate industry and now as the 2009 President of the Florida Association
of Realtors. How did we get to a place where we've got this historic "wave of

commercial debt" headed our way combined with the worst economic crisis since the depression, and a commercial real estate industry that really didn't feel it until 2009?

Cynthia Shelton: I would say we just didn't see it coming. 2008 was my second worst year of my career in real estate; the first was in 1984 when I relocated from Washington State to Florida. I had $65 to $75 million in my pipeline with several projects. And all, except a few of those, fell out in the last quarter of 2008 all due to financing or the market.

Two of the properties were large chain grocery–anchored centers that they occupied and had options to purchase. They changed their minds, due to the uncertainty of the market and to preserve cash. Even though people still need to buy groceries, what they were finding in this particular market, people were moving out of the area, the planned/permitted homes were not being built. At the same time they noticed around the state that people were not buying the high-ticket grocery items with the high-profit margins but were buying hamburger and spaghetti and other staples to get by on. So although sales were strong, profits were not and so expansion slowed as did acquisitions.

TW: What about the ones that failed due to financing? What type of financing were they looking for?

CS: They were looking for non-recourse with 70 and 80 percent loan to value. The last quarter of 2008 banks didn't know which end was up. Quotes changed hourly, and we couldn't count on even those being good. The banks were so scared of what was going on and it was like the whole market was frozen in time. Lenders couldn't lend because they didn't know what to quote on. That's where people started asking: What is going on in the market? Should we just hang on to our properties? Should we pull back and keep our cash?

TW: Did the financing change from one point to the other?

CS: Yes. The financing changed on one deal because the buyer thought he could get in with 25 to 30 percent down, and he was told he had to put 40 percent down. The project went out at $16.5 million, and then went under contract at $15.5 million; the contract fell out because the buyer could not get his financing at 80 percent loan to value. The seller went to contract with someone else at $14.5 million. Again, the buyers had trouble getting their financing. The financing got delayed and did not close by the end of the year. After the first of the year the deal got retraded again, the buyer found financing, but it had to be at an even lower price because the lender didn't think the value was there anymore. In a six-month to seven-month timeframe, we dropped $4 million.

TW: Which equates to around 25 percent decline in value in six months?
CS: That's right. It ended up closing at $11.5 million. The cap rate started at a 7 and closed north of a 9 percent. We also ended up with tenants wanting reductions in their rents. This was happening across the board and not just at this location.

TW: So what do you think happened in the last five years to cause this? When you look at your industry, when you look at your marketplace, do you feel it's just a normal cycle? Because a lot of people feel it's very different this time.
CS: You know, I do think it's another boom-and-bust cycle. I think the boom this time lasted so much longer than people thought it would last. There was almost an artificial feeling that this was the new normal. I can remember in 2007, my partner (Mike Milano) and I talking to some developers and telling the developers "your rental rates are very high for this particular market." What happened was we were seeing rental rates in local shop space with an anchor that had gone from $30 per square foot (sq ft) annually to $38 per sq ft. We had seen that in California, but in Florida those rates had been $18, $19, $20, to $22 per sq ft annually. If you reached $24 per sq ft, you were getting high. Then, over a couple of years rents went from $18 to $24, to $28 to $38 per sq ft annually. That was a very substantial increase.

The landlords had artificially inflated rental values. Then we coupled these high rental rates with very low 5.5 to 6.5 percent cap rates. The prices per sq ft for the buildings went from $250 to $450 per sq ft. Developers were thinking, "Wow! I can build for $100 to $200 per sq ft and sell for $450 per sq ft. Then the tenant's triple net costs got higher and higher as property taxes and insurance skyrocketed. As property taxes increased, sometimes the tenant's share of property taxes was equal to the rent itself.

All of a sudden you're saying, this can't continue. What's happened in the last year or two is now starting to impact us here. Commercially the property taxes are still based on the 6-cap deal from years past. As the proper tax assessments get adjusted for the decline in commercial property values, the cities are going to say, "Wow! We must cut services." It is a downward spiral as our friends from California tell us. California is feeling the impact of budgets as property values were inflated and now the values are dropping. Property taxes are dropping too, thus budgets get out of whack.

TW: So what is going to happen now? In Orlando there were only a few closed sales of retail properties in all of 2009.
CS: We are getting calls from special servicers of the commercial loans to review values, and many of the properties are not worth the debt on them. The other side of it is how long will it take to come out of this cycle? Because

some of the banks are afraid they won't make it through another cycle. If they are forced to start marking these properties to the actual market values, many banks would not make it.

TW: So, it looks like we are going to be in the business of working for banks, in a lot of ways.

CS: We'll be working for the government who is bailing out these banks. I can foresee it having to do that, and I don't like it. We are going to have to rethink how we do things. We need to "retrench" and decide how to make money in this new marketplace.

Dealing with 6-cap deals . . . is just not going to happen. You are fooling yourself and wasting your time. And, you are wasting the owner's time. So you know when you start thinking about hanging on in this market you have to think of reality of what is really the true market. That's probably the big piece of the puzzle.

TW: It sounds like what you are saying is we need to be honest with ourselves and educate ourselves first as a broker, and then educate our clients with that knowledge.

CS: Yes. I think we are just getting to that point. We can't be afraid of alienating a client or losing a listing. We've got to be straightforward even if it means we lose a client. At the end of the day, all we have to sell is our expertise and our time. The lenders are also going to need our help. Residential lenders take discounts for all cash buyers in the residential properties they have taken back in foreclosure. They are going to do the same with commercial properties. Lenders have to accept cash really quick, turn it around to get the markdown off their books. What can they do? I have some clients right now and I have said to them, "Your only hope is that you go in on bended knees and try to get off the hook so you don't lose everything; maybe there is a way to work it out with the lender." And my client replied, "Cynthia, we don't even know where to begin." That's where we could help. However, until the banks realize there is a problem and that we might be able to help them and they let us in, it will be hard. Commercial loans have master servicers, special servicers, investors who own only one-hundredth of the action; it's really going to be tough on a borrower who needs a workout.

If the banks are local, they may be able to actually go in and talk to someone who might be able to assist or find a workout solution.

As brokers we will have to focus on what we know best. I know Florida and I know retail properties. I don't know California and/or industrial properties. We need to learn to say let me get you in the right direction, refer it to someone you know. Learn to say, "We will do our best" to help you but don't overpromise and underdeliver. It is not easy being a broker today when you are juggling many balls trying to make a living. Stay focused.

I did not pretend ever. If I needed a partner, I always took one on. I was the student and he was the teacher or vice versa, sometimes I knew what I was doing, but I wanted a partner. Know your limitations and your strengths. You don't have to give up a piece of business to work on something you are not an expert on; you can partner up with people, other brokers with different areas of expertise. But, don't go out and do something when you know you aren't the expert in that end of the business.

Look, it is scary right now in commercial real estate industry. I am starting to see more and more people who are in worse shape than they thought they were in. Individual ownerships, developers, brokers, and brokerage companies are finding out how bad it really is. The strong can look themselves in the mirror and know that everything is not hunky-dory—and it's not—but the strong ones who stick to basics, scale back on expenses, and work hard who will survive this cycle. And you know what, real estate didn't change overnight: many just thought it did.

Showing Up on Radar

CHAPTER 3

Phase Three: Drawdown (2009)

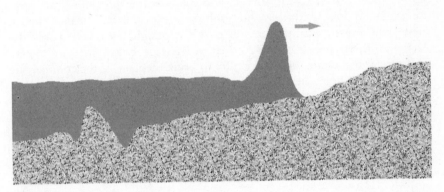

FIGURE 3.1 Drawdown Phase

WATCHING THE WATER RECEDE

The Drawdown phase is a very critical one as it is the last warning before the wave hits (Figure 3.1). In this chapter you will see the commercial real estate market data equivalent of the Drawdown phase for the commercial real estate tsunami.

CoStar Group Inc and its subsidiary, CoStar Realty Information, Inc., one of the preeminent sources of analytical data for the commercial real estate industry, provided me unfettered access to its major metro market data and analytical resources for this book. CoStar Group's massive database includes detailed information on 3.2 million properties totaling just under 65 billion square feet, with 8.7 billion square feet of available space and property listings totaling more than $1 trillion in total value that Tim Trainor, Communications Director, CoStar Group, Inc., reported. To demonstrate the Drawdown taking place in commercial real estate markets across the nation, I have extrapolated the key factors for commercial real estate sales volume, values, vacancy, and rental rates. The consistency of the trends speaks for itself. Indications are these trends will continue in the months and years ahead. An ongoing damage assessment resulting from the wave we are anticipating will be required as the impact and residual effects take place within the commercial real estate sector and related markets.

Earlier in the book I referred to macro numbers related to national trends. In this Phase, the Drawdown, we will look at the numbers in greater detail, separated into major metropolitan markets throughout the United States. These CoStar Group surveys and charts will help demonstrate how the tsunami of loan maturities and resulting foreclosures will further impact these areas already weakened by the overall economic crisis. The Foresight Analytics report previously referenced in Chapter 1 was one of the first commercial real estate reports of 2009 to bring the issue of the commercial debt maturities to public awareness. The *Wall Street Journal* is one of many national financial news organizations that referred to Foresight Analytics as its source on the commercial debt maturity crisis. Matthew Anderson, a partner of Foresight Analytics, directs our attention to the markets that saw the most activity during the boom. He states, "In our view, the risk is spread pretty broadly in terms of both geography and product type, though the areas/types that were most active in 2006 and 2007 would of course be most at risk."

It's clear from the CoStar data and all the other voluminous market reports out there that the wave of commercial real estate foreclosures will not be prejudiced to property type. Generally, you can see that office, hospitality, and retail are obvious victims of the economic downturn, and the economic conditions combined with their debt maturities will only further deteriorate their already weakened values. However, industrial and multi-family will not be exempt from the impact of these conditions. Commercial real estate will be more sensitive to individual attributes to retain or protect values, making it much more difficult to apply the same rules for market valuation and site assessment used over the last 30 years. Each property type and market area will require more individualized evaluation with emphasis on accurate data on the properties, the areas they are located in, and physical and fiscal condition.

The next chapter will discuss the final phase of a tsunami, which is called the Run-up. This is when the swell surges forward, inundating everything in its path until its momentum ebbs and then slowly recedes. Also in the next chapter Dr. Sam Chandan of Real Estate Econometrics does an excellent job reviewing the overall picture of the commercial debt crisis and what measures are being taken to alleviate some of the damage. Based on the research and statistical findings, we would anticipate this Run-up to begin in 2010 and impact the commercial real estate markets through 2013 and possibly longer. While it's impossible to predict precisely when the wave will hit, which areas will be affected, or how devastating the impact will be, there's little doubt the numbers will be historic in terms of commercial real estate mortgage defaults and foreclosures. It is likely we will see a repeat of the patterns set by the residential sector collapse, with several waves of foreclosures before the stabilization and recovery of values can begin.

MAJOR METRO MARKET DATA SURVEYS FROM COSTAR REALTY INFORMATION, INC.

The following is the result of detailed analysis for major metro markets throughout the United States. We have incorporated the CoStar Realty Information data into tables and figures to demonstrate the consistency of the Drawdown phenomena in each market.

Arizona: Phoenix Region

TABLE 3.1   Comparison Report for Arizona: Phoenix Region

PHOENIX REGION
Commercial Real Estate Sales: 2008 versus 2009

Office			
Sales Statistics	2008	2009	% Change
Volume*	$1,340.87	$316.16	−76.42%
Transactions	430	258	−40.00%
Price/SF	$224.94	$131.97	−41.33%
CAP	6.05%	8.77%	44.96%

Retail			
Sales Statistics	2008	2009	% Change
Volume*	$1,669.74	$1,067.96	−36.04%
Transactions	351	211	−39.89%
Price/SF	$183.94	$151.52	−17.63%
CAP	6.86%	8.48%	23.62%

Industrial			
Sales Statistics	2008	2009	% Change
Volume*	$1,081.72	$455.35	−57.91%
Transactions	381	195	−48.82%
Price/SF	$83.93	$74.34	−11.43%
CAP	6.92%	13.42%	93.93%

*Volume is in millions

Source: Market data derived from CoStar Realty Information, Inc. and subject to copyright.

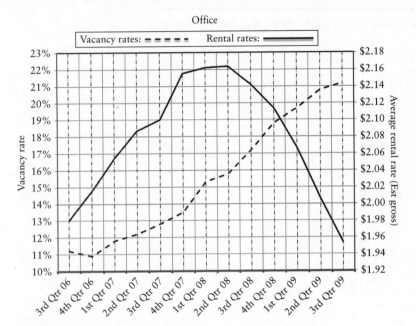

FIGURE 3.2A   Phoenix Region, Vacancy and Rental Rates: Office

Source: Market data derived from CoStar Realty Information, Inc. and subject to copyright

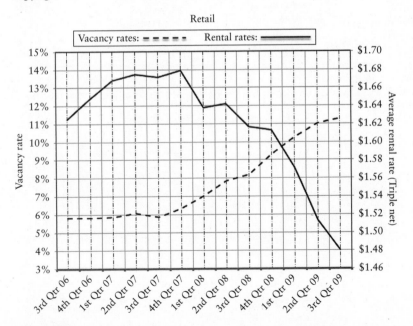

FIGURE 3.2B   Phoenix Region, Vacancy and Rental Rates: Retail

Source: Market data derived from CoStar Realty Information, Inc. and subject to copyright

California: Los Angeles-Orange County Region

TABLE 3.2   Comparison Report for California: Los Angeles–Orange County Region

LOS ANGELES REGION
Commercial Real Estate Sales: 2008 versus 2009

Sales Statistics	Office		
	2008	2009	% Change
Volume*	$4,479.74	$1,272.27	–71.60%
Transactions	669	371	–44.54%
Price/SF	$314.82	$216.26	–31.31%
CAP	5.83%	7.60%	30.36%

Sales Statistics	Retail		
	2008	2009	% Change
Volume*	$3,705.01	$1,327.34	–64.17%
Transactions	1289	841	–34.76%
Price/SF	$269.94	$253.62	–6.05%
CAP	5.98%	6.72%	12.37%

Sales Statistics	Industrial		
	2008	2009	% Change
Volume*	$3,287.00	$1,483.38	–54.87%
Transactions	1076	641	–40.43%
Price/SF	$128.15	$104.72	–18.28%
CAP	6.02%	11.95%	98.50%

*Volume is in millions
Source: Market data derived from CoStar Realty Information, Inc. and subject to copyright.

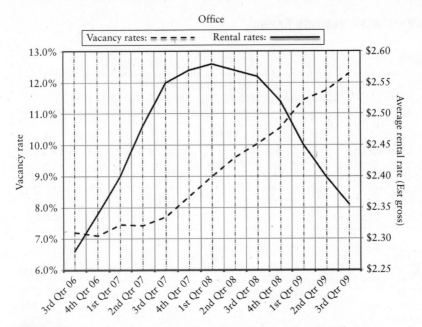

FIGURE 3.3A Los Angeles Region, Vacancy and Rental Rates: Office

Source: Market data derived from CoStar Realty Information, Inc. and subject to copyright

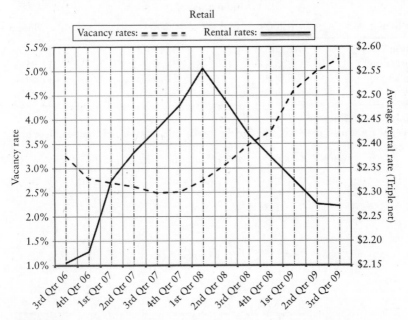

FIGURE 3.3B Los Angeles Region, Vacancy and Rental Rates: Retail

Source: Market data derived from CoStar Realty Information, Inc. and subject to copyright

California: Sacramento Region

TABLE 3.3 Comparison Report for California: Sacramento Region

SACRAMENTO REGION
Commercial Real Estate Sales: 2008 versus 2009

Office

Sales Statistics	2008	2009	% Change
Volume*	$413.07	$192.11	−53.49%
Transactions	151	103	−31.79%
Price/SF	$237.50	$193.67	−18.45%
CAP	7.28%	6.74%	−7.42%

Retail

Sales Statistics	2008	2009	% Change
Volume*	$1,100.95	$211.28	−80.81%
Transactions	177	134	−24.29%
Price/SF	$162.05	$168.75	4.13%
CAP	6.89%	8.67%	25.83%

Industrial

Sales Statistics	2008	2009	% Change
Volume*	$380.71	$247.71	−34.93%
Transactions	153	98	−35.95%
Price/SF	$78.50	$110.72	41.04%
CAP	6.93%	8.46%	22.08%

*Volume is in millions

Source: Market data derived from CoStar Realty Information, Inc. and subject to copyright.

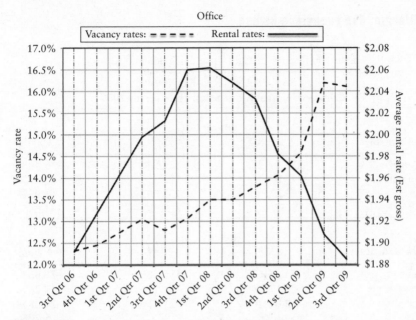

FIGURE 3.4A   Sacramento Region, Vacancy and Rental Rates: Office

Source: Market data derived from CoStar Realty Information, Inc. and subject to copyright

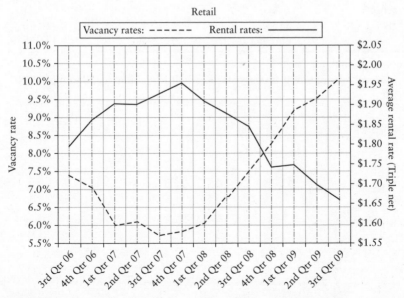

FIGURE 3.4B   Sacramento Region, Vacancy and Rental Rates: Retail

Source: Market data derived from CoStar Realty Information, Inc. and subject to copyright

California: San Francisco Region

TABLE 3.4   Comparison Report for California: San Francisco Region

SAN FRANCISCO REGION
Commercial Real Estate Sales: 2008 versus 2009

Sales Statistics	Office 2008	2009	% Change
Volume*	$2,169.55	$642.13	−70.40%
Transactions	201	115	−42.79%
Price/SF	$329.98	$323.62	−1.93%
CAP	5.57%	7.31%	31.24%

Sales Statistics	Retail 2008	2009	% Change
Volume*	$1,256.37	$305.89	−75.65%
Transactions	253	174	−31.23%
Price/SF	$210.58	$253.50	20.38%
CAP	5.66%	6.55%	15.72%

Sales Statistics	Industrial 2008	2009	% Change
Volume*	$1,213.26	$1,079.33	−11.04%
Transactions	268	142	−47.01%
Price/SF	$138.77	$123.92	−10.70%
CAP	5.68%	13.50%	137.68%

*Volume is in millions
Source: Market data derived from CoStar Realty Information, Inc. and subject to copyright.

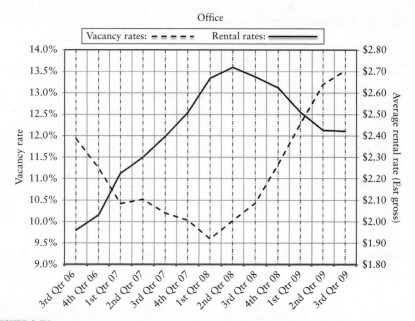

FIGURE 3.5A San Francisco Region, Vacancy and Rental Rates: Office

Source: Market data derived from CoStar Realty Information, Inc. and subject to copyright

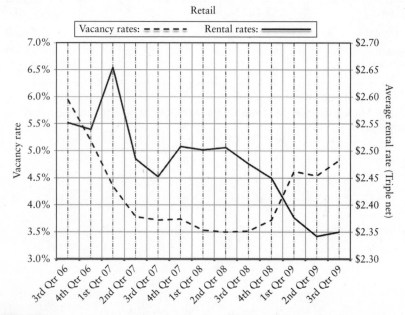

FIGURE 3.5B San Francisco Region, Vacancy and Rental Rates: Retail

Source: Market data derived from CoStar Realty Information, Inc. and subject to copyright

Colorado: Denver Region

TABLE 3.5　Comparison Report for Colorado: Denver Region

DENVER REGION
Commercial Real Estate Sales: 2008 versus 2009

Office			
Sales Statistics	2008	2009	% Change
Volume*	$1,345.66	$247.35	−81.62%
Transactions	418	147	−64.83%
Price/SF	$159.78	$122.62	−23.26%
CAP	6.59%	8.59%	30.35%

Retail			
Sales Statistics	2008	2009	% Change
Volume*	$1,048.65	$281.39	−73.17%
Transactions	498	237	−52.41%
Price/SF	$177.60	$123.64	−30.38%
CAP	7.31%	8.05%	10.12%

Industrial			
Sales Statistics	2008	2009	% Change
Volume*	$882.75	$458.97	−48.01%
Transactions	525	235	−55.24%
Price/SF	$63.72	$73.03	14.61%
CAP	7.36%	13.32%	80.98%

*Volume is in millions
Source: Market data derived from CoStar Realty Information, Inc. and subject to copyright.

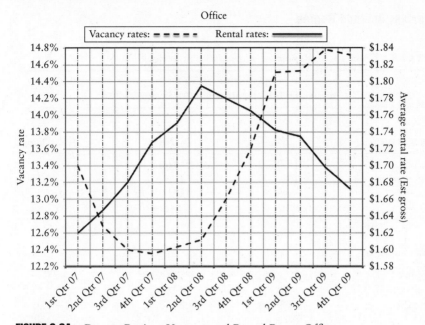

FIGURE 3.6A   Denver Region, Vacancy and Rental Rates: Office

Source: Market data derived from CoStar Realty Information, Inc. and subject to copyright

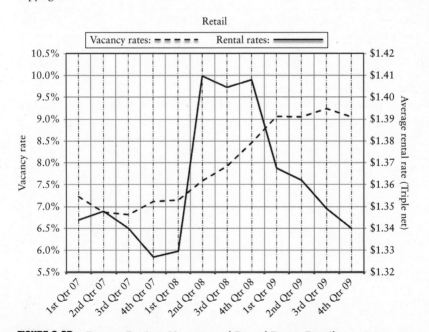

FIGURE 3.6B   Denver Region, Vacancy and Rental Rates: Retail

Source: Market data derived from CoStar Realty Information, Inc. and subject to copyright

Florida: Orlando Region

TABLE 3.6   Comparison Report for Florida: Orlando Region

ORLANDO REGION
Commercial Real Estate Sales: 2008 versus 2009

Sales Statistics	Office 2008	2009	% Change
Volume*	$429.32	$168.24	−60.81%
Transactions	182	136	−25.27%
Price/SF	$194.99	$160.40	−17.74%
CAP	6.92%	8.48%	22.54%

Sales Statistics	Retail 2008	2009	% Change
Volume*	$1,264.27	$184.17	−85.43%
Transactions	218	148	−32.11%
Price/SF	$158.64	$156.91	−1.09%
CAP	7.19%	7.70%	7.09%

Sales Statistics	Industrial 2008	2009	% Change
Volume*	$559.82	$853.57	52.47%
Transactions	163	89	−45.40%
Price/SF	$70.93	$84.34	18.91%
CAP	6.97%	13.62%	95.41%

*Volume is in millions
Source: Market data derived from CoStar Realty Information, Inc. and subject to copyright.

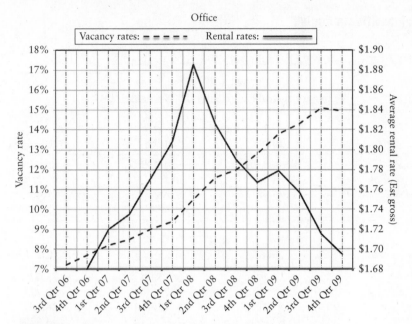

FIGURE 3.7A   Orlando Region, Vacancy and Rental Rates: Office

Source: Market data derived from CoStar Realty Information, Inc. and subject to copyright

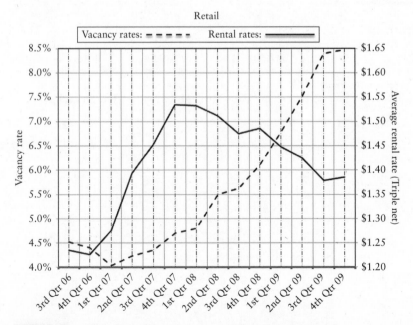

FIGURE 3.7B   Orlando Region, Vacancy and Rental Rates: Retail

Source: Market data derived from CoStar Realty Information, Inc. and subject to copyright

Georgia: Atlanta Region

TABLE 3.7 Comparison Report for Georgia: Atlanta Region

ATLANTA REGION
Commercial Real Estate Sales: 2008 versus 2009

Sales Statistics	Office 2008	2009	% Change
Volume*	$2,303.28	$243.39	−89.43%
Transactions	497	282	−43.26%
Price/SF	$164.02	$96.06	−41.43%
CAP	7.72%	7.93%	2.72%

Sales Statistics	Retail 2008	2009	% Change
Volume*	$2,622.83	$655.08	−75.02%
Transactions	705	432	−38.72%
Price/SF	$157.42	$112.43	−28.58%
CAP	7.37%	7.88%	6.92%

Sales Statistics	Industrial 2008	2009	% Change
Volume*	$1,257.02	$905.52	−27.96%
Transactions	448	241	−46.21%
Price/SF	$45.17	$33.25	−26.39%
CAP	7.51%	7.89%	5.06%

*Volume is in millions
Source: Market data derived from CoStar Realty Information, Inc. and subject to copyright.

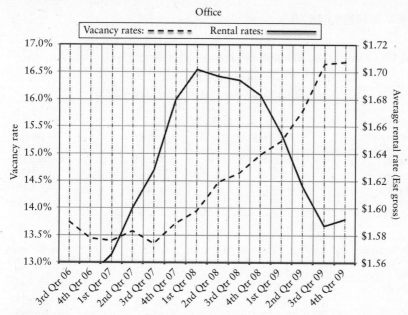

FIGURE 3.8A   Atlanta Region, Vacancy and Rental Rates: Office

Source: Market data derived from CoStar Realty Information, Inc. and subject to copyright

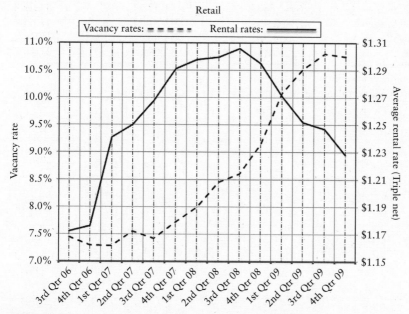

FIGURE 3.8B   Atlanta Region, Vacancy and Rental Rates: Retail

Source: Market data derived from CoStar Realty Information, Inc. and subject to copyright

Illinois: Chicago Region

TABLE 3.8   Comparison Report for Illinois: Chicago Region

CHICAGO REGION
Commercial Real Estate Sales: 2008 versus 2009

Sales Statistics	Office		
	2008	2009	% Change
Volume*	$2,352.67	$792.31	−66.32%
Transactions	493	252	−48.88%
Price/SF	$167.83	$137.56	−18.04%
CAP	8.57%	8.02%	−6.42%

Sales Statistics	Retail		
	2008	2009	% Change
Volume*	$2,981.44	$770.05	−74.17%
Transactions	1078	628	−41.74%
Price/SF	$203.85	$125.88	−38.25%
CAP	7.03%	8.45%	20.20%

Sales Statistics	Industrial		
	2008	2009	% Change
Volume*	$2,382.89	$1,556.15	−34.69%
Transactions	802	420	−47.63%
Price/SF	$53.75	$44.42	−17.36%
CAP	7.36%	8.96%	21.74%

*Volume is in millions
Source: Market data derived from CoStar Realty Information, Inc. and subject to copyright.

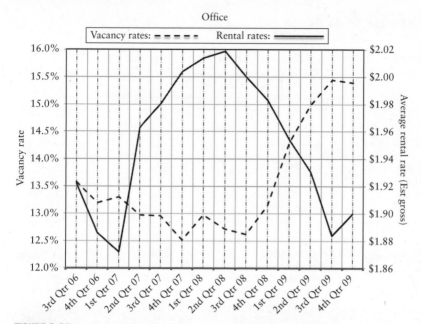

FIGURE 3.9A Chicago Region, Vacancy and Rental Rates: Office

Source: Market data derived from CoStar Realty Information, Inc. and subject to copyright

FIGURE 3.9B Chicago Region, Vacancy and Rental Rates: Retail

Source: Market data derived from CoStar Realty Information, Inc. and subject to copyright

Nevada: Las Vegas Region

TABLE 3.9   Comparison Report for Nevada: Las Vegas Region

LAS VEGAS REGION
Commercial Real Estate Sales: 2008 versus 2009

Sales Statistics	Office 2008	2009	% Change
Volume*	$637.49	$90.06	−85.87%
Transactions	113	69	−38.94%
Price/SF	$207.14	$185.39	−10.50%
CAP	6.92%	7.86%	13.58%

Sales Statistics	Retail 2008	2009	% Change
Volume*	$1,586.46	$148.38	−90.65%
Transactions	146	62	−57.53%
Price/SF	$222.03	$161.00	−27.49%
CAP	7.21%	8.83%	22.47%

Sales Statistics	Industrial 2008	2009	% Change
Volume*	$373.17	$242.23	−35.09%
Transactions	133	40	−69.92%
Price/SF	$128.69	$105.67	−17.89%
CAP	6.33%	13.22%	108.85%

*Volume is in millions
Source: Market data derived from CoStar Realty Information, Inc. and subject to
copyright.

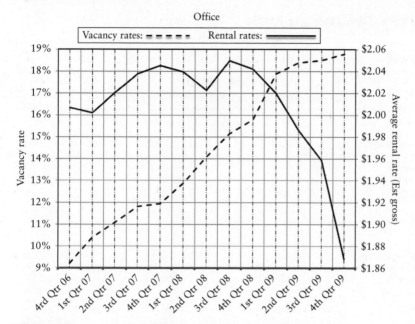

FIGURE 3.10A Las Vegas Region, Vacancy and Rental Rates: Office

Source: Market data derived from CoStar Realty Information, Inc. and subject to copyright

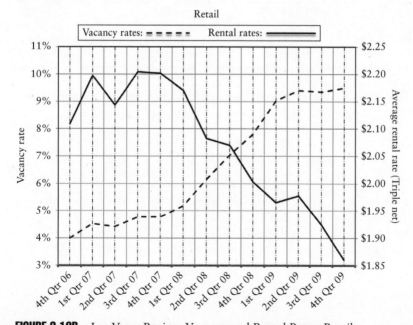

FIGURE 3.10B Las Vegas Region, Vacancy and Rental Rates: Retail

Source: Market data derived from CoStar Realty Information, Inc. and subject to copyright

New York: New York City Region

TABLE 3.10   Comparison Report for New York: New York City Region

NEW YORK REGION
Commercial Real Estate Sales: 2008 versus 2009

Sales Statistics	Office 2008	2009	% Change
Volume*	$13,661.34	$2,401.63	−82.42%
Transactions	172	99	−42.44%
Price/SF	$738.67	$386.67	−47.65%
CAP	4.41%	5.45%	23.58%

Sales Statistics	Retail 2008	2009	% Change
Volume*	$2,299.04	$550.59	−76.05%
Transactions	199	68	−65.83%
Price/SF	$880.01	$649.17	−26.23%
CAP	5.60%	6.15%	9.82%

Sales Statistics	Industrial 2008	2009	% Change
Volume*	$135.97	$10.07	−92.59%
Transactions	18	4	−77.78%
Price/SF	$371.63	$481.14	29.47%
CAP	NA	NA	

*Volume is in millions
Source: Market data derived from CoStar Realty Information, Inc. and subject to copyright.

FIGURE 3.11A New York Region, Vacancy and Rental Rates: Office

Source: Market data derived from CoStar Realty Information, Inc. and subject to copyright

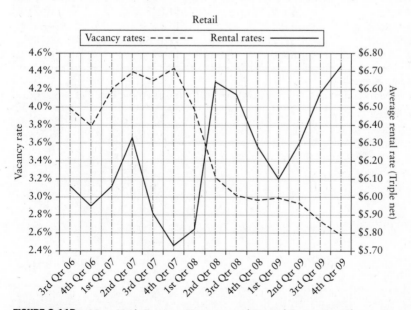

FIGURE 3.11B New York Region, Vacancy and Rental Rates: Retail

Source: Market data derived from CoStar Realty Information, Inc. and subject to copyright

Oregon: Portland Region

TABLE 3.11   Comparison Report for Oregon: Portland Region

PORTLAND REGION
Commercial Real Estate Sales: 2008 versus 2009

Office			
Sales Statistics	**2008**	**2009**	**% Change**
Volume*	$781.35	$241.04	−69.15%
Transactions	188	116	−38.30%
Price/SF	$199.22	$125.60	−36.95%
CAP	7.07%	7.97%	12.73%

Retail			
Sales Statistics	**2008**	**2009**	**% Change**
Volume*	$385.14	$232.34	−39.67%
Transactions	213	221	3.76%
Price/SF	$184.02	$125.19	−31.97%
CAP	7.01%	8.44%	20.40%

Industrial			
Sales Statistics	**2008**	**2009**	**% Change**
Volume*	$329.30	$1,023.29	210.75%
Transactions	159	152	−4.40%
Price/SF	$77.59	$101.56	30.89%
CAP	6.43%	13.87%	115.71%

*Volume is in millions
Source: Market data derived from CoStar Realty Information, Inc. and subject to copyright.

FIGURE 3.12A   Portland Region, Vacancy and Rental Rates: Office

Source: Market data derived from CoStar Realty Information, Inc. and subject to copyright

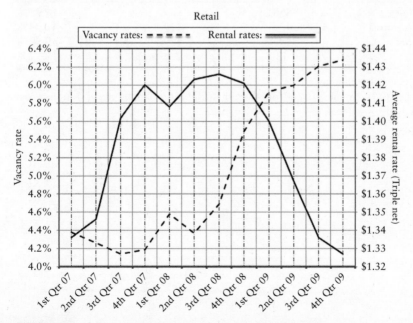

FIGURE 3.12B   Portland Region, Vacancy and Rental Rates: Retail

Source: Market data derived from CoStar Realty Information, Inc. and subject to copyright

Texas: Dallas–Ft. Worth Region

TABLE 3.12   Comparison Report for Texas: Dallas-Fort Worth Region

DALLAS-FORT WORTH REGION
Commercial Real Estate Sales: 2008 versus 2009

Sales Statistics	Office 2008	2009	% Change
Volume*	$1,637.41	$273.48	−83.30%
Transactions	397	247	−37.78%
Price/SF	$147.47	$62.81	−57.41%
CAP	6.46%	8.08%	25.08%

Sales Statistics	Retail 2008	2009	% Change
Volume*	$1,309.30	$923.43	−29.47%
Transactions	757	633	−16.38%
Price/SF	$150.54	$151.56	0.68%
CAP	7.59%	7.72%	1.71%

Sales Statistics	Industrial 2008	2009	% Change
Volume*	$858.29	$697.36	−18.75%
Transactions	541	319	−41.04%
Price/SF	$49.45	$29.70	−39.94%
CAP	8.48%	9.49%	11.91%

*Volume is in millions
Source: Market data derived from CoStar Realty Information, Inc. and subject to copyright.

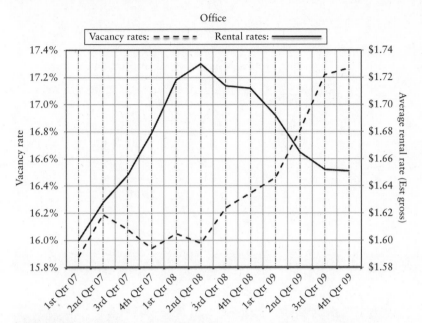

FIGURE 3.13A Dallas-Ft. Worth Region, Vacancy and Rental Rates: Office

Source: Market data derived from CoStar Realty Information, Inc. and subject to copyright

FIGURE 3.13B Dallas-Ft. Worth Region, Vacancy and Rental Rates: Retail

Source: Market data derived from CoStar Realty Information, Inc. and subject to copyright

CHAPTER 4

Phase Four: The Run-Up (2010–2013)

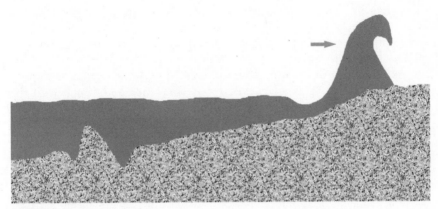

FIGURE 4.1   Run-Up Phase

The Run-Up phase of a tsunami is the last stage of the wave as it makes its final approach to the shoreline and infiltrates deep inland, creating havoc and destruction as it washes over land (see Figure 4.1). The wave's powerful force and momentum, combined with its sudden arrival, give it tremendous damage potential. As we see in the excerpts from the following congressional testimony from the real estate industry's leadership, building a wall of protection from the approaching tsunami will be a daunting task. The challenge for solutions demands creativity, leadership, and commitment from the commercial real estate industry, governmental agencies, and Congress alike to follow through for years to come.

RECOGNIZING THE POTENTIAL HAVOC IN THE MARKET

On July 9, 2009, the first important congressional hearing was held in Washington, DC, with a panel from the commercial real estate and lending industry. The composition of the panel chosen to testify before the hearing demonstrated the imperative nature of the urgent message to Congress. Real Estate Roundtable, National Association of Realtors, representatives of Deutsche Bank (reporting on their findings related to CMBS), and Jon D. Greenlee, Associate Director, Division of Banking Supervision and Regulation Board of Governors of the Federal Reserve all came to the hearing with clear intentions to inform and warn Congress as to what kinds of actions were needed and the possible ramifications if nothing was done. While I was only going to present excerpts from the panel's testimony in this book, the statements are so informative that I felt compelled to include their testimony in its entirety. To watch the actual hearing testimony, a link will be posted at www.tonywoodconsulting.com, and it is worth every bit of the 30 or so minutes it takes to watch.

As I watched the hearing I was impressed with the legitimate inquiry by members of Congress; however, I was concerned and struck with the impression that they were just getting up to speed with the depth of the problems we are facing in the commercial real estate industry. Questions like, "Is this truly a systemic problem that, if not addressed, will have implications beyond the commercial real estate sector?" The answers reflected a unanimous, "Yes!" What followed was the equivalent of, "What if we do nothing?" I cringed as I heard this type of question, knowing what the possible ramifications could be nationwide. The answers from the panel to this question were ominous. The hearing presented an interesting question that neither I nor my associates have heard asked before in my 34-plus years in the commercial real estate industry: What percentage of the Gross National Product is represented by the commercial real estate industry? The resulting answer from Jeffrey DeBoer, President and CEO of the Real Estate Roundtable, was approximately 13 percent. This answer clearly made a deep impression on those members of Congress in the hearing and their concerns for action were transformed to asking what they could do to help. It became clear the emerging commercial real estate crises could in fact thwart our economy's fledgling recovery. Something had to be done, but where do they start?

The statements submitted by the panel members that follow in this chapter will show that we do have some good people working on these matters. Solutions are being investigated, and regulatory actions are being formulated and implemented. However, what these statements also demonstrate is the complexity of the problems and the multifaceted areas of the commercial real estate industry that need attention. All sectors of the commercial real estate industry—commercial lenders, owners, borrowers with commercial real estate loans, and commercial real estate brokers—need to get involved with the process and ensure that industry associations and congressional representatives are aware of the concerns and suggestions for solving the problems at hand.

The Real Estate Roundtable Statement provides a comprehensive description of the overall picture and actual proposals for solutions to some of the problems presented the commercial real estate market faces today. Unfortunately, many of the proposed solutions will face tough resistance, such as major tax law changes. Moreover, there are solutions yet to be proposed for the multitude of problems small businesses, owner-users, and smaller portfolio investors and commercial lenders will be facing. This is one of the issues highlighted in Dr. Sam Chandan's chapter, "Bailing Out a Sea of Debt" which follows next.

EXCERPTS FROM CONGRESSIONAL TESTIMONY

The Real Estate Roundtable

STATEMENT OF JEFFREY D. DEBOER ON BEHALF OF THE REAL ESTATE ROUNDTABLE, UNITED STATES CONGRESS JOINT ECONOMIC COMMITTEE HEARING ON COMMERCIAL REAL ESTATE: DO RISING DEFAULTS POSE A SYSTEMIC THREAT?

RAYBURN HOUSE OFFICE BUILDING ROOM 2226 WASHINGTON, DC

Thursday, July 9, 2009

Introduction

Thank you, Chairman Maloney, Vice Chairman Schumer, Ranking Members Brady and Brownback, members of the Committee, for conducting today's hearing on the state of the economy with respect to commercial real estate.

I am Jeffrey DeBoer, and I am the President and Chief Executive Officer of The Real Estate Roundtable, an organization that represents the leadership of the nation's top 130 privately owned and publicly held real estate ownership, development, lending, and management firms, as well as the elected leaders of the 16 major national real estate industry trade associations. Collectively, Roundtable members hold portfolios containing over 5 billion square feet of developed property valued at over $1 trillion, over 1.5 million apartment units, and in excess of 1.3 million hotel rooms. Participating Roundtable trade associations represent more than 1.5 million people involved in virtually every aspect of the real estate business.

Thank you for the opportunity to testify today about the impact the economic downturn and credit market dislocation is having on commercial real estate and how that dislocation will negatively affect the overall economy and impede future economic growth.

By way of background, when I speak of the commercial real estate sector I am speaking of six principal property types—apartment, office, retail, industrial, health care, and hotels. It is also important to realize that the commercial real estate market includes many diverse regional and local markets, as well as submarkets within markets, each with their own dynamics. A common attribute through all, however, is that they each depend on a healthy economy for occupancy and operating income, and on a liquid financing market to facilitate investment, development, and sales of properties.

My message today is simple and straightforward. The current credit system in America simply does not have the capacity to meet the legitimate demand for commercial real estate debt. As the demands for debt remain unmet, the stress to the financial services system overall, individual financial institutions, and those who have invested in real estate directly or indirectly will increase.

The lack of credit has stalled transaction volume, which has fallen by nearly 80 percent. Asset values are estimated to have fallen from their peak by approximately 35 percent on average, and capitalization rates are presumed to have increased by approximately 250 basis points, while rents have declined up to 20 percent depending on the property type. Yet, with a scarcity of property transactions, there is no effective price discovery, and this further exacerbates the real estate credit market crisis—where loan-to-value is a critical metric used in the lending process. This is a market failure of catastrophic proportions.

With very limited capacity to meet the ongoing demand for credit, there is increasing concern about a potential wave of defaults—from maturing loans—that will further exacerbate the current credit crisis. Needless to say, this has broad systemic consequences and will reverse the progress that has been made in healing the banking system and credit markets to date.

What Does This Mean for Main Street USA?

The commercial real estate sector of the economy is large, representing $6.7 trillion of value supported by $3.5 trillion in debt. Its health is vital to the economy (estimates show commercial real estate constitutes 13 percent of GDP by revenue) and our nation's financial system.

An estimated 9 million jobs are generated or supported by real estate—jobs in construction, planning, architecture, environmental consultation and remediation, engineering, building maintenance and security, management, leasing, brokerage, investment and mortgage lending, accounting and legal services, interior design, landscaping, cleaning services, and more.

Rising defaults (resulting from a lack of refinancing options) and falling property values in commercial real estate will create a cascade of negative repercussions for the economy as a whole.

- **For millions of Americans whose pension funds invest directly or indirectly in approximately $160 billion of commercial real estate equity,** increased loan defaults and lower property values will mean a smaller retirement nest egg.
- **For millions of construction, hotel, and retail workers,** the commercial real estate liquidity vacuum will translate into cancelled or delayed projects, layoffs, and pinched family budgets—exacerbating rising unemployment and declining consumer spending. This, in turn, will further hurt U.S. businesses and exacerbate falling demand for commercial real estate space.
- **For state and local governments,** erosion of property values will mean less revenue from commercial property assessments, recording fees, and transaction taxes resulting in bigger budget shortfalls.
- **For the communities they serve,** it will mean cutbacks in essential public services such as education, road construction, law enforcement, and emergency planning.

I am here today to continue to sound the alarm bell. The policy actions to date have been helpful, but additional steps are called for to help transition the ownership and financing of commercial real estate from a period of higher than desirable leverage and weak loan underwriting to a time of systemically supportable leverage, sounder underwriting, and economic growth.

As detailed below, we recommend that the following policy actions should be enacted as soon as possible:

1. Extend the Term Asset-Backed Securities Loan Facility (TALF) beyond its current December 31, 2009 sunset date, through the end of 2010.
2. Establish a federally backed credit facility, possibly created from the Public Private Investment Program (PPIP) structure or a privately funded guarantee program, for originating new commercial real estate loans.
3. Encourage foreign capital investment in U.S. real estate by amending or repealing the outdated Foreign Investment in Real Property Tax Act (FIRPTA).
4. Encourage banks and loan servicers to extend performing loans, based on cash flow analysis; and, temporarily amend real estate mortgage investment conduit (REMIC) regulations to facilitate early review and possible modification to the terms of commercial mortgage loans that have been securitized in CMBS.
5. Reject new anti-real estate investment taxes, such as the carried interest proposal, and provide a five-year carry-back for the net operating losses of all businesses.

The Current Picture

The commercial real estate industry is in deep stress for two reasons. First, the macro economy is caught in a "Great Recession": Unemployment is high and likely going higher; consumer spending is down substantially; and business and personal travel is down. All of which results in reduced operating income for property owners and lower property values.

Second, and in many respects more importantly, the credit markets are essentially closed to refinancing existing real estate debt or securing new debt to facilitate transactions. The lack of a functioning credit market is putting further downward pressure on property values and is causing many commercial property owners to face "maturity defaults" on their loans. This will create a great deal of added stress on the banking system, as losses are absorbed, and on the overall economy.

The size of the problem is large today and if not addressed could become large enough to undermine the positive economic growth signs that are starting to appear. Commercial real estate in America is valued at approximately $6.7 trillion. It is supported by about $3.5 trillion of debt (see Figure 4.2).

Most commercial real estate debt has loan terms of ten years or less, and therefore a significant percentage of outstanding debt matures each year and needs to be refinanced. The three largest providers of credit to the sector are (1) commercial banks, with $1.5 trillion, or 43 percent; (2) commercial mortgage backed securities (CMBS) accounts for approximately $750 billion, or 22 percent; and (3) life insurance companies, with $315 billion or 9 percent. Additionally, some $330 billion is held by the government-sponsored enterprises (GSEs), agencies, or GSE-backed mortgage pools (see Figure 4.3).

In 2009, the amount of maturing commercial real estate loans is estimated to be between $300 and $500 billion. Maturing debt in this sector continues to expand. With an average $400 billion of commercial real estate debt maturities each year for the next decade,

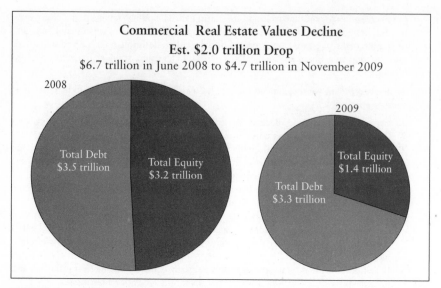

FIGURE 4.2   Commercial Real Estate Debt and Equity

Note: Est. value of investment-grade income-producing real estate. 2009 value decline estimates range from NCREIF RI of 28.25% to Moody's/REALCPPI of 40.55%. 2009 chart assumes 30% overall decline, with 90% attributed to equity and 10% debt. 2008 Data Source: JPMorgan Asset Management

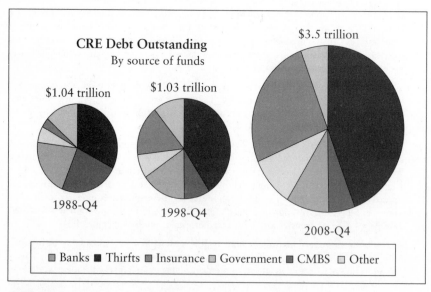

FIGURE 4.3   CRE Debt Outstanding

Source: Federal Reserve Flow of Funds Accounts of the United States

the credit market as it is currently structured does not have the capacity to absorb this demand (see Figure 4.4).

During the last several years, banks and the commercial mortgage-backed securities market provided about 83 percent of the growth in commercial real estate debt. Today both of these large sources of commercial real estate credit are virtually shut down.

The CMBS market is illustrative of the problem. CMBS issuance peaked in 2007 with $230 billion of bonds issued; this plunged to $12 billion in 2008—a nearly 95 percent decline. Thus far this year, there has been no new CMBS issuance (see Figure 4.5).

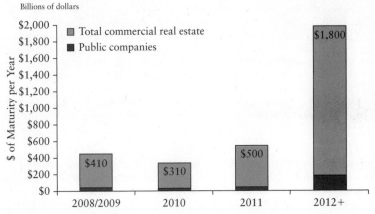

FIGURE 4.4 Commercial Real Estate Debt Maturities
Source: Goldman Sachs and REIT filings

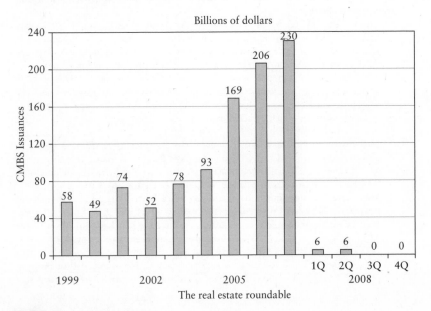

FIGURE 4.5 CMBS Issuance

The result is that the $6.7 trillion commercial real estate sector, a very large contributor to overall economic growth, now faces a liquidity crisis of mammoth proportions—where even performing loans, on strong assets in good markets, face extreme difficulty in refinancing their debt.

That being said, it is noteworthy that real estate investment trusts (REITs) and other publicly traded real estate companies have raised appreciable amounts of equity, as well as some debt, so far in 2009 as investors have sought opportunities to deploy capital in the more liquid and transparent sectors of the market. Since the beginning of the year, REITs, which represent approximately 10 percent of the overall commercial real estate market, have raised nearly $16.3 billion in the public equity markets and approximately $2.4 billion of unsecured debt. These capital-raising activities alone do not mean that commercial real estate is out of the woods. The industry overall continues to face tremendous challenges to maintain sufficient liquidity in the face of the current credit crisis. But, it is definitely a positive sign that some capital has been made available through public securities markets to the publicly traded segment of the commercial real estate business. The only other sources of credit available to the sector are the government-sponsored enterprises—Fannie Mae and Freddie Mac—but these sources are limited to the multifamily market. So, additional measures are imperative on the credit front in order to further reduce financial pressures for all owners and operators of commercial real estate.

Policy Actions Are Needed

We appreciate the steps taken so far by the Congress, the Federal Reserve, and the Treasury Department to try to address the vast liquidity crisis that is crippling the economy, destroying jobs, and causing a free fall in commercial property values. But much more needs to be done. We suggest policymakers focus on the following principal areas.

1. **Even if portfolio lenders—such as commercial banks and life companies—returned to the market in force, these institutions simply do not have the capacity to satisfy demand. Therefore, steps must be taken to restore an active commercial mortgage securitization market.**
    - **We are encouraged by the creation of the Term Asset-Backed Loan Facility (TALF), which will provide attractive financing to investors who purchase newly issued AAA-rated securities backed by commercial real estate loans.** Newly issued AAA-rated commercial mortgage backed securities (CMBS) became eligible for TALF financing in late June, as will legacy AAA CMBS later in July. This program is intended to help reconnect the loan originators with the secondary markets. This program already has been very helpful in addressing the liquidity problem in consumer debt—such as auto loans and credit card debt—and has led to the issuance of nearly $51 billion of financing. For example, newly issued AAA-rated asset-backed securities (ABS) were recently priced through TALF at a spread of 155 basis points over LIBOR. That's 100 basis points less than where the market would have priced it, and approximately 400 basis points better than where similar securities were trading at the end of 2008 (see Figure 4.6).
    - **We believe that, once it is fully functioning for real estate later in the summer, this program will be helpful to commercial real estate as well.** The Federal Reserve Board's recent announcement regarding the much-anticipated expansion of the TALF program to legacy CMBS assets brought an even stronger market reaction than when the announcement of the new issue parameters came out. The extension of eligible TALF collateral to include legacy CMBS is intended to promote price discovery and liquidity for legacy CMBS. However, there are concerns that

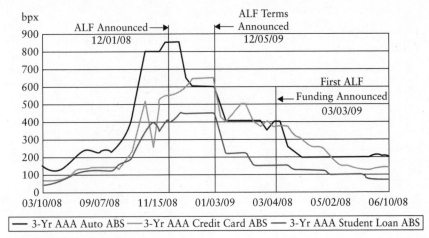

FIGURE 4.6 ABS Treasury Spreads
Source: The Real Estate Roundtable

a recent watch listing by Standard & Poor's of many of the potentially qualified legacy securities could limit the eligibility of most potential legacy CMBS bonds for TALF funding.

■ For example, since the TALF announcement, risk premiums on the top-rated AAA portions of securities with recent loans as collateral have tightened by 650 basis points over Treasuries from a high of 1350 basis points in November of 2008. The resulting improvement in legacy CMBS markets should ultimately facilitate the issuance of newly issued CMBS, thereby helping borrowers finance new purchases of commercial properties or refinance existing commercial mortgages on better terms (see Figure 4.7).

■ We support the Federal Reserve's recent move to expand the list of acceptable credit rating agency firms from three to five. This should introduce more competition among the firms and provide investors with a better view of the performance of existing CMBS. Moreover, we have long supported reform of the credit rating agencies. Along those lines, the SEC took long overdue steps recently to increase the transparency of the credit rating agencies' rating methodologies, strengthen their disclosure, prohibit them from engaging in practices that create conflicts of interest, and enhance their record keeping and reporting obligations. This action should provide increased confidence to the investor community regarding the strength of underlying securities.

■ However, due to the long lead time necessary to assemble TALF-eligible CMBS transactions, the program's remaining term does not permit adequate time to develop sufficient volume to address the massive credit shortfall to the sector. For this reason, we strongly recommend that the Federal Reserve extend the TALF beyond its current December 31, 2009 deadline, through the end of 2010. If not, only a very limited number of CMBS securitizations will take place under TALF,

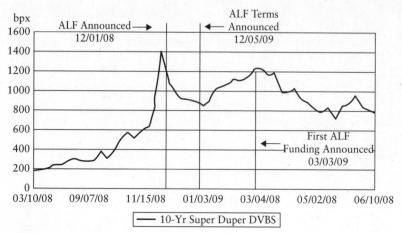

FIGURE 4.7　Super Duper CMBS Treasury Spread
Source: The Real Estate Roundtable

and the program will end before it has had the desired effect on price discovery and a return of an active securitization market.

- **While the TALF is intended to help restart a segment of the CMBS securitization market, it is no panacea.** While the leverage the TALF provides to investors in the AAA-rated securities is attractively priced, it is cost-prohibitive to add debt over the AAA-rated piece due to the frozen credit markets. As a result, the program effectively gives the market 35 to 45 percent loan-to-value financing. Historically, conservatively underwritten loans were in the 60 percent loan-to-value range. More typically, loans were extended to 75 percent loan-to-value levels. With a drop in collateral asset values of, say, 35 percent, this makes loan-to-value a critical concern. So, only a very narrow segment of the market will be eligible for TALF-based commercial real estate loans. TALF will not be a significant help to the vast bulk of maturing CMBS loans that need to be refinanced, and it will not solve the over-leverage issues affecting the major segment of the market.

- **The TALF's reliance on the credit rating agencies to assess valuation is a concern.** Due to a scarcity of sale transactions, there is no true "market" for property level commercial real estate assets. As a result, values are extremely difficult to ascertain. In an environment where these agencies are struggling to regain their credibility with investors, the credit rating agencies will likely be compelled to value the collateral at a relatively low level, compared to historic norms. The resulting AAA-rated piece will likely be a relatively small portion of the overall financing available to borrowers. The result of this is that TALF will not be able to meet the current demand from maturing commercial real estate loans.

- **We also support the Public Private Investment Program (PPIP) announced by the Treasury and other regulators.** This program will also provide attractive financing to private investors to purchase legacy or toxic assets held by financial institutions.

Removing these assets should help to enable banks to return to the business of making sound loans to commercial real estate. While we are concerned about the postponement of the Legacy Loans Program by the Federal Deposit Insurance Corporation (FDIC), we are encouraged by reports that the Treasury will soon be announcing their selection of asset management firms to participate in the program. The PPIP will use matching federal money and funds raised by the selected companies from private investors to buy distressed mortgage-backed securities and other troubled assets from U.S. banks. The purchases are intended to establish market prices for the assets, clean up bank balance sheets, and revitalize lending.

2. **Additional steps must be taken to facilitate "new" real estate loan originations:**
   - We have been studying the creation of a federally chartered, privately funded loan guarantee program for commercial real estate securities. After an initial period of support from TARP and the Federal Reserve (similar to the TALF program), such a program would be self-funded by a fee charged to the issuers of securities—in much the same way the Federal Deposit Insurance Corporation insures bank deposits. Such an entity would create an insurance pool to stand behind these securities and help restore investor confidence and restart securitization markets. While our interest is in focusing such an entity on the CMBS market, it could be used for a variety of asset classes. By creating a loan guarantee facility for newly issued mortgage-backed securities, banks and loan originators will have a stable secondary market into which they can sell newly originated, solidly underwritten loans.
   - Another option we have been pursuing would involve the adaptation of the PPIP's public-private investment structure under the stalled Legacy Loans Program (LLP). Under this structure, Public Private Investment Funds (PPIFs) would be created, utilizing private capital with leverage from the federal government. However, instead of using the program for so-called legacy—or troubled—loans, the PPIFs would be used to fund a pipeline of solidly underwritten, *newly* originated commercial real estate loans. Instead of acquiring legacy loans, the program would shift to new loans and provide an important source of liquidity to the industry at the whole loan level. It would also help solve the warehousing problems afflicting potential TALF-eligible CMBS loan originators.
   - Finally, non-U.S. investors could provide significant new real estate lending originations if the Treasury and the Internal Revenue Service would issue a Notice (or other guidance) to confirm that real estate loan originations are encompassed by the proprietary securities trading safe harbor of section 864(b)(2) of the Tax Code and thus such actions do not constitute a U.S. trade or business. Clarifying this would expand real estate lending capacity in the country and enable non-U.S. investors to originate real estate debt just as they are now allowed under current tax law to invest in existing debt.

3. **Given the lack of liquidity, regulators must give lenders and mortgage servicers more flexibility to restructure loans and make modifications when a positive outcome can be generated. It is also important for bank regulators to establish policies—possibly in the form of guidance—that would temporarily encourage banks to extend existing loans that are current—where there is adequate debt service coverage to service debt payments.**
   - As part of this effort, it is important to amend the real estate mortgage investment conduit (REMIC) rules to facilitate reasonable modifications to the terms of commercial mortgage loans that have been securitized in CMBS. The current administrative tax rules applicable to REMICs and investment trusts exacerbate

the problem by imposing limitations that significantly impede the ability to negoti-ate and implement a restructuring package on a timely basis. To that end, the Real Estate Roundtable has requested that the Treasury Department issue guidance that would temporarily suspend the current administrative tax rules that, in normal economic conditions; serve to restrict the ability to restructure securitized mort-gage loans. We are hopeful that Treasury will act soon in this important area.

■ In the banking sector, since long-term value is hard to determine in the current environment, bank regulations should temporarily encourage banks to extend existing loans where there is adequate debt service to cover payments. Such guid-ance would also encourage banks to focus on cash flow and debt service coverage and minimize dependence on loan-to-value measurements. This could help mini-mize costly foreclosures and help alleviate the pressure on banks to reduce their commercial real estate exposure.

4. Because of the significant value declines in commercial real estate—estimated by some to be 35% or more—for lending to resume, and transactions to go forward, there must be significant additional equity investment into the market place. Preliminary conserva-tive estimates reveal an "equity gap" exceeding $1 trillion over the next several years. One potential source for this needed equity investment is foreign pension and other non-U.S. fund pools—but policy must facilitate this investment (see Figure 4.8).

■ In the best interest of the economy, the Congress should make a much-needed policy change by modifying the Foreign Investment in Real Property Tax Act ("FIRPTA").

■ As you may know, under current U.S. tax law, gains realized from the sale of U.S. real estate by non-U.S. investors are subjected to U.S. taxation at full U.S. rates under the Foreign Investment in Real Property Tax Act of 1980 ("FIRPTA"). Such taxation is completely at odds with the U.S. tax treatment of a large number of other types of foreign investments in the United States. With a few technical exceptions, FIRPTA is literally the only major provision of U.S. tax law [that] subjects non-U.S. investors to taxation on capital gains realized from investment in U.S. assets. By modifying FIRPTA, non-U.S. investors will be encouraged to inject much-needed capital into the U.S. real estate markets.

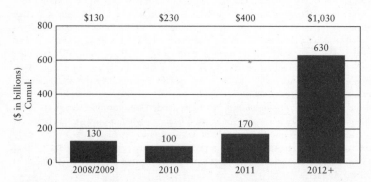

FIGURE 4.8   Required Equity for Commercial Real Estate Debt Maturities

Note: Assumes conservative valuation decline of 20%, original LTV of 70% and refinancing LTV of 60%. Required equity increases if value decline is higher or LTV is lower.

- Over the years, FIRPTA has had an adverse effect on foreign investment in U.S. real estate. In fact, the obstacles that are imposed under FIRPTA have led many non-U.S. investors to invest in real estate elsewhere—to such countries as Brazil, China, and India—shifting wealth and economic dynamism away from the U.S. market. The laws relating to foreign investment in U.S. real estate should be reviewed by Congress and corrected in a responsible way to allow increased investment into U.S. real estate, while still ensuring that the real estate is domestically controlled (see Figure 4.9).

5. **Now is not the time to pursue new anti-real estate investment taxes such as increasing the capital gains rate or the proposed tax hike on partnership "carried interest."** Both these ideas are anti-investment and should be set aside at least until the economy rights itself. And, all businesses should be made eligible for the five-year carry-back of net operating loses

    - **The "carried interest" proposal is sometimes discussed as a potential "revenue raiser" but would be a very negative policy change now.** It would significantly raise taxes on a broad range of commercial and multifamily real estate owners of all sizes and property types. The proposal frequently is portrayed simply as a tax increase on a few well-heeled "hedge fund" and private equity managers and as a move toward tax fairness. This could not be further from the truth.

    - In fact, it would impose a huge tax increase on countless Americans who use partnership structures for all types and sizes of businesses. It would be especially bad for real estate businesses.

    - An increase in this tax rate would be the first time that the sweat equity of an entrepreneur who is building a business would be taxed as ordinary income. The carried interest tax would dampen, if not stifle, entrepreneurial activity. A higher tax on entrepreneurial risk-taking will have a chilling effect on investment. It would discourage risk-taking that drives job creation and economic growth. In short, it would have profound unintended consequences for Main Street America. Now is the time to create jobs, not destroy them.

    - Enacting this proposal would be playing Russian roulette with an economy that is already weak in the knees. Taxing carried interest at ordinary income rates is not sound economic practice, especially given the current economic crisis. Instead of encouraging equity investment, the proposal would encourage real estate owners to borrow more money to avoid taking on equity partners,

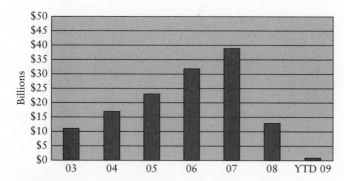

FIGURE 4.9 Foreign Investment in U.S. Real Estate

thereby delivering a huge blow to the 1.5 million workers directly employed in the real estate business and the nation's 800,000 construction workers. These are outcomes the Administration should be trying to avoid at this critical point in the recession.

■ About 15 million Americans are partners in more than 2.5 million partnerships. They manage nearly $12 trillion in assets and generate roughly $400 billion in annual income. Virtually every real estate partnership, from the smallest apartment venture to the largest investment fund, has a carried interest component. Through these structures, entrepreneurs match their ideas, know-how, and effort with equity investors. Taxing all carried interests in partnerships as ordinary income would be a whopping 150 percent tax increase. As much as $20 billion in value annually could be driven from the economy.

■ Further, 46 percent of all partnerships are engaged in real estate, and 60 percent of their income is capital gain[s] income. Real estate general partners put "sweat equity" into their business, fund the predevelopment costs, guarantee the construction budget and financing, and expose themselves to potential litigation over countless possibilities. They risk much. Their gain is never guaranteed. It is appropriately taxed today as capital gain.

■ Regarding net operating loss (NOL) carry-back, the NOL provision is one of the strongest tools Congress can provide to help companies in a broad cross-section of industries weather the current economic conditions. Faced with limited access to capital, the ability to transform a future tax benefit into cash today is critical to maintain otherwise viable businesses. As you are aware, Congress provided a five-year carry-back for 2001 and 2002 NOLs and AMT NOL relief to companies of all sizes in the *Job Creation and Worker Assistance Act of 2002* enacted following the September 11 terrorist attacks.

Currently, the NOL provision that was enacted into law by the *American Recovery and Reinvestment Act* provided a five-year carry-back for 2008 NOLs, but arbitrarily limited the relief to small companies with annual gross receipts of $15 million or less. As a proven economic stimulus tool, the NOL provision should be expanded to mid to large size companies, which currently are limited to a two-year allowance for tax years beginning or ending in 2008 and 2009. For many in the commercial real estate industry, the five-year NOL carry-back could provide the capital they need to bridge the gap until the other previously mentioned stimulative measures have an opportunity to work.

Conclusion

In summary, conditions in the nation's commercial real estate markets today are quite challenging. Property fundamentals are sliding due to weakness in the overall economy.

Defaults and foreclosures are expected to increase due to the paralyzed credit markets. Together, the resulting value declines and debt dislocations threaten to undermine any nascent economic stabilization some believe is now underway.

The overriding concern lies in the credit markets. Here, it is important that government continue to take appropriate steps, along the lines of the TALF and PPIP, to restore functionality to credit markets and create an environment conducive for business and investors to invest and deploy capital. At the same time, it is important that unnecessary barriers to equity investment be lowered and that taxes on risk taking not be increased.

We encourage Congress and the Administration to pursue such measures or a combination of measures that could be rapidly implemented and help address this catastrophic situation. We stand ready to discuss and aid in the development and implementation of such measures.

Thank you for the opportunity to testify today.

■ ■ ■

The National Association of Realtors©

TESTIMONY OF JAMES HELSEL, PARTNER, RSR REALTORS ON BEHALF OF THE NATIONAL ASSOCIATION OF REALTORS© BEFORE U.S. JOINT ECONOMIC COMMITTEE HEARING REGARDING "COMMERCIAL REAL ESTATE: DO RISING DEFAULTS POSE A SYSTEMIC THREAT?"

July 9, 2009

Introduction

Chairman Maloney, Vice Chairman Schumer, Ranking Members Brady and Brownback, and Members of the Joint Economic Committee, thank you for inviting me to testify today on the crisis facing the commercial real estate markets. My name is Jim Helsel, and I am a Partner with RSR Realtors, a full-service real estate company in Harrisburg, PA. I have been involved in real estate for 34 years and currently serve as the 2009 Treasurer of the National Association of Realtors©.

I am here to testify on behalf of more than 1.1 million Realtors who are involved in residential and commercial real estate as brokers, sales people, property managers, appraisers, counselors, and others engaged in all aspects of the real estate industry. Members belong to one or more of 1,400 local associations/boards and 54 state and territory associations of Realtors. Realtors thank the Joint Economic Committee for holding this very important hearing to examine the myriad of severe problems facing the commercial real estate industry.

Overall State of the Commercial Real Estate Markets

Having a sound and well-functioning commercial and multifamily real estate sector is critical to our country's economic growth and development and to millions of U.S. businesses of all sizes that provide local communities with jobs and services. It is estimated that the commercial real estate sector supports more than 9 million jobs and generates billions of dollars in federal, state, and local tax revenue. Nonetheless, the overall economic downturn and crisis in the broader financial markets is directly impacting not only the fundamentals of commercial real estate finance, but also the outlook for recovery. And while the commercial and multifamily real estate markets play a vital role in the economy, these markets are now experiencing the worst liquidity challenge since the early 1990s.

Many of us in commercial real estate have been warning for some time that the liquidity crisis facing our industry has the potential to wreak havoc on the broader economy. In fact, an apt description for the situation is that commercial real estate is the "next shoe to drop." The collapse of the nation's housing market had and continues to have a huge impact on the entire global financial system. Likewise, it is important to recognize the economic ramifications of a widespread collapse in the commercial real estate markets.

Deteriorating property fundamentals, declining property values, and a severe tightening of lending activity are all factors contributing to the current crisis. According to NAR's most recent Commercial Real Estate Outlook report, released in May of this year, " . . . with credit markets contracting in the wake of the financial crisis, businesses also slashed spending. The result has been a major hit for commercial real estate, translated into shrinking demand, growing space availability, and a collapse in the volume of sales. As companies file for bankruptcy and as the ranks of unemployed grow, commercial space finds itself under pressure."

Nowhere is this more evident than in the retail industry. The nation's shopping center owners face a double hit—the economic recession, corresponding unemployment, and reduced consumer confidence mean that consumer spending is down dramatically while at the same time owners and investors face tremendous difficulties in securing financing. According to a recent International Council of Shopping Centers survey of shopping center owners—which represented a cross section of the industry that accounted for over 5,100 shopping centers and 12.6 percent of all shopping center space—62.7 percent of respondents cited little or no confidence in refinancing company debt during 2009. In addition, 53.9 percent held that same opinion for 2010. A recent article in *U.S. News & World Report* entitled "America's Most Endangered Malls" further highlighted the extent of the financial troubles facing distressed retail properties and included some startling data supporting the bleak outlook for America's retail landscape. One statement from the article bears mentioning here—"By some estimates, about 10 percent of America's malls could close within the next few years."

While demand for space is essentially in a state of full retreat, we also see that vacancy rates are climbing across all property types and transaction activity for commercial properties is in a major slowdown. To highlight this critical situation, during the first quarter of 2009, nationwide only 607 major properties exchanged hands, for a total sales volume of $9.5 billion. The figure represents a 51 percent drop in investment activity compared with the fourth quarter 2008.

The decline is evident in each sector of commercial real estate. Based on the first quarter 2009 data, office investments were down 75 percent compared to a year ago, while industrial sales volume declined 83 percent. At the same time, compared with the prior year, apartment investments dropped a significant 85 percent and retail sales contracted 72 percent (see Figure 4.10).

The lack of liquidity and banks' reluctance to extend lending are also becoming apparent in the increasing level of delinquent properties. Delinquencies on commercial loans 30-plus days past due almost doubled from the first quarter of 2006 to the fourth quarter of 2008. Multifamily properties are leading the delinquency wave, with about $24.5 billion of delinquent loans.

Given that property loans are not being refinanced, there is a growing volume of distressed commercial properties. This year, the volume of distressed real estate has more than doubled. Currently, there are over 5,300 commercial properties in default, foreclosure, or bankruptcy. The value of these distressed properties is in excess of $100 billion and rising. The impact is felt across all property types and across all regions of the country, weighing most heavily on the people whose livelihood depends on an economic recovery. In fact, together with retail stores and hotels, apartment buildings are taking the brunt of the refinancing crisis. Together the three sectors account for over 3,500 distressed properties, totaling more than $65 billion dollars. Geographically, New York City presents the largest problem, with Manhattan possessing almost $8 billion of distressed commercial properties. Other markets with large concentrations of distressed commercial real estate are Las Vegas, Los Angeles, Detroit, Phoenix, Chicago, Dallas, and Boston.

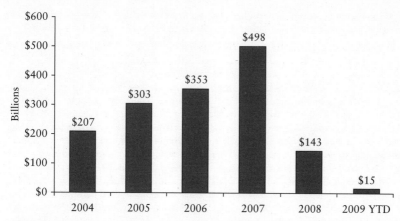

FIGURE 4.10 U.S. Commercial Real Estate Sales Volume
Source: Real Capital Analytics, June 2009

What is alarming to us, as real estate professionals, is that banks' responses to this growing threat have been slow and inadequate. The rate at which these troubled loans are being resolved has been sluggish. Over $60 billion in assets have become distressed this year but only $4 billion worth of commercial loans have been resolved so far.

In addition, commercial banks and the commercial mortgage-backed securities (CMBS) market represent approximately 70 percent of all outstanding commercial real estate loans. However, banks have tightened their credit standards and reduced commercial real estate loan volume while the CMBS market, which has been a key source of liquidity to the commercial sector, has ceased to function. In 2007, a record high of $230 billion of CMBS was issued. In 2008, this figure dropped to $12 billion and thus far in 2009, there has not been a single CMBS issuance. Hundreds of billions of dollars of commercial real estate loans from a variety of sources are expected to mature in 2009 and over $1 trillion by 2012. Under current conditions, there is clearly insufficient credit capacity to refinance this huge wave of loan maturities. Without greater liquidity, commercial borrowers are facing a growing challenge of refinancing maturing debt and the threat of rising delinquencies and foreclosures that could cause widespread damage.

Members' Experiences

Though commercial Realtors around the country are experiencing different types of challenges, depending to a large degree on their local markets and what type of business they focus on, I believe that most commercial practitioners, whether they are involved with retail, office space, or industrial warehouse development, will tell you that the biggest challenge in this environment is the inability to complete transactions due to a severe lack of liquidity in the markets. Underscoring this fact, a full 44 percent of our members reported financing as their most significant current challenge in a recent REALTOR© market survey.

I would like to provide you with several examples submitted to us by commercial realtors from around the country: From a Memphis apartment broker and certified commercial investment specialist (CCIM), "I am now on my fifth contract for the Park Tower apartments in Memphis. It is located across from the VA Hospital in the Medical Center area of Memphis. Four out of five contracts have failed due to the lack of available financing. . . .

Lenders with and without TARP money are saying no before they review the numbers or clients. It is the worst lending market that I have seen in my 25 years in the business."

And this from a commercial realtor in Atlanta who specializes in industrial properties—"We recently bid on an industrial warehouse by the airport. The property was only 25 percent leased, but we were purchasing the property for $6.25 per square foot (probably 80 percent below replacement cost of the potential income stream). In the past, we would have been able to purchase that property with a loan of 75 percent and equity of 25 percent so long as the bank felt we had approached our underwriting and lease up conservatively. We underwrote the property very conservatively, and instead of 75 percent debt, we came with 75 percent equity and asked for a loan of only 25 percent. Our primary bank said no, and several small banks [that] would have typically strongly considered this deal said no. Over the past ten years, we have purchased or developed close to a million square feet of industrial real estate. We have never defaulted on a loan or missed a mortgage payment. Without the ability to get a loan to leverage our potential returns, it is impossible to make real estate deals appealing enough to investors. We are basically out of business until banks start loosening their guidelines."

These are but two examples, and clearly there are thousands more around the country. Each failed transaction, foreclosure, or distressed property creates further pressure and problems with widespread economic repercussions. We have lost about 6.5 million jobs over the past year and a half of economic recession. Many of these jobs have been in office, industrial, retail, and multifamily sectors. A continued increase in distressed commercial properties will result in more job cuts.

Economically, commercial real estate has lagged residential real estate cycles. Even during an economic recovery, commercial real estate continues on a downward trend for a while. The residential real estate sector has been in a severe downturn for over two years. During this time, homeowners have lost over $4 trillion in wealth. Even with some positive recent signs, the residential market is still looking for a bottom. With this relationship in mind, it is obvious that for commercial real estate the worst is yet to come. The length and severity of the downturn along with the accompanying pain to business and consumers depend largely on the credit markets and the banks' willingness to step in and provide financing for properties which are well-capitalized and performing in many cases.

Policy Suggestions

To address the serious problems facing the commercial real estate finance markets, NAR believes that it is imperative that we take proactive steps now to provide liquidity and facilitate lending. We commend Congress, the financial regulators, and the Administration for the development and implementation of several innovative programs and initiatives, such as the Term Asset-Backed Lending Facility (TALF) and the Public Private Investment Program (PPIP). We strongly support several recent moves on the part of Treasury to strengthen the TALF program—for example, expanding TALF to include CMBS as eligible collateral, while also making the terms of TALF loans five years to better accommodate the longer term nature of commercial loans. Nonetheless, the TALF program is set to expire at the end of this year. NAR believes that it is absolutely essential that the TALF program be extended for another year in order to continue to provide the necessary liquidity support to keep economic recovery efforts on track.

NAR also commends the Administration for the development of its comprehensive financial regulatory reform proposal. We truly believe that it is important to have strong supervision and regulation of the nation's financial system. We stand ready to work with policymakers and the Administration in the shaping of this monumental plan, but we also believe that it is essential that reform efforts do not negatively impact the efforts currently underway to revitalize and stabilize the commercial real estate markets, in particular those efforts targeted at the securitization markets.

As previously mentioned, the CMBS market has been a key player in supporting commercial real estate lending, but due to challenging capital market conditions, in the past year the CMBS market has ceased to function. The securitization markets represent an important source of liquidity, and NAR believes that it is essential to protect and promote policies that support the securitized credit markets and do not impede economic recovery.

Along these lines, we believe that actions on the part of the accounting policymakers are critical as part of the overall federal government's efforts to address capital constraints, provide liquidity, and facilitate lending. NAR believes that the ability to value assets in inactive markets continues to be a serious issue, and we urge policymakers to act quickly to provide meaningful and clear guidance so that market participants can effectively address application issues and ensure that "fair value" accounting standards can be achieved and applied consistently for all market conditions. Under current conditions, clear policy guidance is needed to encourage reporting entities and auditors to look to alternative and appropriate methods of asset valuation, such as the discounted cash flow model.

Finally, the intense revenue pressures created by the present economic crisis will undoubtedly drive major tax overhaul efforts. In light of this, NAR will continue to support and promote federal tax policies that strengthen and support commercial real estate. The commercial real estate market is in a state of crisis and remains vulnerable to any modifications to current tax rules that would result in reduced property values. NAR stands ready to oppose any such modifications and would urge policymakers to do the same.

Conclusion

The National Association of Realtors applauds the bold actions that have been taken thus far to address the serious liquidity problems facing commercial real estate finance. Innovative programs and initiatives, such as the TALF and the PPIP, certainly represent part of the solution, but more action is needed. NAR believes that the principles we have set forth today will help Congress and the regulators design a holistic approach that will address the liquidity crisis currently facing the commercial real estate markets.

I thank you for this opportunity to present our thoughts. As always, the National Association of Realtors is at the call of Congress, the financial regulators, and the Administration to help in the ongoing effort to find solutions to stabilize and ensure recovery of the commercial real estate markets. Such an effort is particularly important given that the commercial real estate sector is a key component to job creation and economic revitalization for the nation as a whole.

Again, we appreciate the Committee holding this hearing and we stand ready to assist in any way in your efforts going forward.

■ ■ ■

The Federal Reserve

For release on delivery 10:00 AM EDT July 9, 2009

Statement of Jon D. Greenlee Associate Director, Division of Banking Supervision and Regulation Board of Governors of the Federal Reserve System before the United States Congress Joint Economic Committee Hearing on Commercial Real Estate: Do Rising Defaults Pose a Systemic Threat?

July 9, 2009

Chair Maloney, Vice Chairman Schumer, Ranking Members Brownback and Brady, and other members of the Committee, I am pleased to be here today to discuss several issues related to commercial real estate (CRE) lending in the United States. I will start by describing the current conditions in CRE markets, then discuss Federal Reserve efforts to help revitalize CRE markets and promote lending to creditworthy borrowers. I will also outline Federal Reserve supervisory actions relating to CRE and discuss the need to ensure a healthy balance between strong underwriting, risk management, and financial institution safety and soundness on the one hand, and credit availability, on the other.

Current Conditions in CRE and CMBS Markets

Financial market dislocations and the continuing economic downturn are clearly challenging CRE markets. The pace of property sales has slowed dramatically since peaking in 2007, from quarterly sales of roughly $195 billion to about $20 billion in the first quarter of 2009. Demand for commercial property is sensitive to trends in the labor market, and, as job losses have accelerated, tenant demand for space has declined and vacancy rates have increased.

The decline in the CRE market has been aggravated by two additional factors. First, the values of commercial real estate increased significantly between 2005 and 2007, driven by many of the same factors behind the residential housing bubble, resulting in many properties either purchased or refinanced at inflated values. Prices have declined about 24 percent since their peak in the fall of 2007, and market participants expect significant further declines. Second, the market for securitized commercial mortgages (CMBS), which accounts for roughly one-fourth of outstanding commercial mortgages, has been largely dormant since early 2008 while many banks have substantially tightened credit. The decline in property values and higher underwriting standards in place at banks will increase the potential that borrowers will find it difficult to refinance their maturing outstanding debt, which often includes substantial balloon payments.

The higher vacancy levels and significant decline in value of existing properties have also placed pressure on new construction projects. As a result, the construction market has experienced sharp declines in both the demand for and the supply of new construction loans since peaking in 2007.

The negative fundamentals in the commercial real estate property markets have broadly affected the credit performance of loans in banks' portfolios and loans in commercial mortgage backed securities. At the end of the first quarter of 2009, there was approximately $3.5 trillion of outstanding debt associated with commercial real estate. Of this, $1.8 trillion was held on the books of banks, and an additional $900 billion represented collateral for CMBS. At the end of the first quarter, about 7 percent of commercial real estate loans on banks' books were considered delinquent. This was almost double from the level a year earlier. The loan performance problems were the most striking for construction and land development loans, especially for those that finance residential development. Notably, a high proportion of small and medium-sized institutions continue to have sizable exposure to commercial real estate, including land development and construction loans, built up earlier this decade, with some having concentrations equal to several multiples of their capital.

The Federal Reserve's Senior Loan Officer Opinion Survey regularly provides useful information about lending conditions. In the most recent survey, conducted in April of this year, almost two-thirds of the domestic banks surveyed reported having tightened standards and terms on commercial real estate loans over the previous three months. Additionally, almost two-thirds of the respondents reported weaker demand for CRE loans, the highest net percentage so reporting since the survey began tracking demand for CRE loans in April 1995.

The current fundamentals in CRE markets are exacerbated by a lack of demand for CMBS, previously a financing vehicle for about 30 percent of originations. New CMBS issuance has come to a halt as risk spreads widened to prohibitively high levels in response to the increase in CRE specific risk and the general lack of liquidity in structured debt markets. There has been virtually no new issuance since the middle of 2008. Increases in credit risk have significantly softened demand in the secondary trading markets for all but the most highly rated tranches of these securities. Delinquencies of mortgages in CMBS have increased markedly in recent months, and market participants anticipate these rates will climb higher by the end of this year, driven not only by negative fundamentals but also borrowers' difficulty in rolling over maturing debt. In addition, the decline in CMBS prices has generated significant stresses on the balance sheets of institutions that must mark these securities to market.

Federal Reserve Activities to Help Revitalize CRE Markets

U.S. government agencies have taken a number of actions to strengthen the financial sector and to promote the availability of credit to businesses and households. In addition to aggressive actions related to monetary policy, the Federal Reserve has taken strong actions to improve liquidity in financial markets by establishing numerous liquidity facilities. One of the more recent liquidity programs is the Term Asset-Backed Securities Loan Facility (TALF), begun in November 2008, to facilitate the extension of credit to households and small businesses. In an effort to target CMBS markets, in May of this year, the Federal Reserve announced that, starting in June 2009, certain newly issued high-quality CMBS would become eligible collateral under the Loans 30 or more days past due.

TALF [was] followed in July by high quality "legacy" CMBS issued before January 1, 2009. The provision of TALF financing for newly issued CMBS was intended to support new lending for creditworthy properties, especially those whose loans are set to mature soon. TALF financing for legacy CMBS was intended to lower secondary market spreads and enhance liquidity. Lower spreads should then encourage new lending and ease the balance sheet pressures on owners of CMBS. The resulting improvement in CMBS markets should facilitate the issuance of new CMBS, thereby helping borrowers finance new purchases of commercial properties or refinance existing commercial mortgages on better terms.

TALF loans will be offered to finance new issuances of CMBS and purchases of legacy CMBS once a month. No TALF loans collateralized by new CMBS have been made yet, in part because CMBS take some time to arrange. The first subscription to include legacy CMBS will be on July 16, 2009.

Federal Reserve Supervisory Activities Related to CRE

The Federal Reserve has been focused on commercial real estate (CRE) exposures at supervised institutions for some time. As part of our supervision of banking organizations in the early 2000s, we began to observe rising CRE concentrations. Given the central role that CRE lending played in the banking problems of the late 1980s and early 1990s, we led an interagency effort to issue supervisory guidance on CRE concentrations in 2006. In that guidance, we emphasized our concern that some institutions' strategic- and capital-planning processes did not adequately acknowledge the risks from their CRE concentrations. We stated that stress testing and similar exercises were necessary for institutions to identify the impact of potential CRE shocks on earnings and capital, especially the impact from credit concentrations.

As weaker housing markets and deteriorating economic conditions have impaired the quality of CRE loans at supervised banking organizations, we have devoted significantly more supervisory resources to assessing the quality of regulated institutions' CRE portfolios. These efforts include monitoring carefully the impact that declining collateral values may have on institutions' CRE exposures as well as assessing the extent to which banks have been complying with the interagency CRE guidance. Reserve Banks with geographic areas suffering more acute price declines in real estate have been particularly focused on evaluating exposures arising from CRE lending. We have found, through horizontal reviews and other examination activities, that many institutions would benefit from additional and better stress testing, improved management information systems, and stronger appraisal practices, and that some banks need to improve their understanding of how concentrations—both single-name and sectoral/geographical concentrations—can impact capital levels during shocks.

The recently concluded Supervisory Capital Assessment Process (SCAP) provides a perspective of the risks of CRE exposures. The nineteen firms reviewed in the SCAP had over $600 billion in CRE loans, of which more than half were for non-farm/non-residential properties, and about one-third were related to construction and land development. The SCAP estimated that cumulative two-year CRE losses under the adverse scenario, in which residential house prices would continue to fall dramatically in 2009 and 2010, would be more than 8 percent of total CRE exposures, with losses on construction loans significantly higher. Using information gained from the SCAP simulation exercise, we are also working with smaller firms that have substantial CRE exposures to ensure that their risk management practices are adequate and that they continue to maintain appropriate reserves and capital to support an expected increase in CRE losses.

As part of our ongoing supervisory efforts related to CRE, we implemented additional examiner training so that our examiners are equipped to deal with more serious CRE problems at both community and regional banking organizations on a consistent basis. Further, we have enhanced our outreach to key real estate market participants and obtained additional market data sources to help support our supervisory monitoring activities. We have also issued guidance to our examiners on real estate appraisals, proper use of interest reserves in construction and development loans, evaluation of loan loss reserving methodologies, and troubled debt restructuring practices.

Maintaining Balance in the Supervisory Process

The Federal Reserve has long-standing policies and procedures in place to promote institutions' risk identification and management practices that support sound bank lending and the credit intermediation process. In fact, guidance issued in 1991, during the last commercial real estate crisis, specifically instructs examiners to ensure that regulatory policies and actions do not inadvertently curtail the availability of credit to sound borrowers. The 1991 guidance also states that examiners are to ensure that supervisory personnel are reviewing loans in a consistent, prudent, and balanced fashion.

The 1991 guidance covers a wide range of specific topics, including the general principles that examiners follow in reviewing commercial real estate loan portfolios, the indicators of troubled real estate markets, projects, and related indebtedness, and the factors that examiners consider in their review of individual loans, including the use of appraisals and the determination of collateral value. Credit classification guidelines were also addressed.

This emphasis on achieving an appropriate balance between credit availability and safety and soundness continues and applies equally to today's CRE markets. Consistent with the 2006 CRE guidance, institutions that have experienced losses, hold less capital, and are operating in a more risk-sensitive environment are expected to employ appropriate risk-management practices to ensure their viability. At the same time, it is important that supervisors remain balanced and not place unreasonable or artificial constraints on lenders that could hamper credit availability.

As part of our effort to help stimulate appropriate bank lending, the Federal Reserve and the other federal banking agencies issued regulatory guidance in November 2008 to encourage banks to meet the needs of creditworthy borrowers. The guidance was issued to encourage bank lending in a manner consistent with safety and soundness—specifically, by taking a balanced approach in assessing borrowers' ability to repay and making realistic assessments of collateral valuations.

More generally, we have directed our examiners to be mindful of the pro-cyclical effects of excessive credit tightening. Across the Federal Reserve System, we have implemented training and outreach to underscore these intentions. We are mindful of the potential for bankers to overshoot in their attempt to rectify lending standards and want them to understand that it is in their own interest to continue making loans to creditworthy borrowers.

Conclusion

Financial markets in the United States continue to be somewhat fragile, with CRE markets particularly so. Banking institutions have been adversely impacted by recent problems in CRE markets. The Federal Reserve, working with the other banking agencies, has acted—and will continue to act—to ensure that the banking system remains safe and sound and is able to meet the credit needs of our economy. We have aggressively pursued monetary policy actions and provided liquidity to help repair the financial system. The recent launch of the CMBS portion of the TALF is an effort to revitalize lending in broader CRE markets. In our supervisory "Interagency Policy Statement on the Review and Classification of Commercial Real Estate Loans" (November 1991); www.federalreserve.gov/boarddocs/srletters/1991/SR9124.HTM [and] "Interagency Statement on Meeting the Needs of Credit Worthy Borrowers" (November 2008); www.federalreserve.gov/newsevents/press/bcreg/20081112a.htm efforts, we are mindful of the risk-management deficiencies at banking institutions revealed by the current crisis and are ensuring that institutions develop appropriate corrective actions. Within the Federal Reserve, we have been able to apply our interdisciplinary approach to addressing problems with CRE markets, relying on supervisors, economists, accountants, quantitative analysts, and other experts.

It will take some time for the banking industry to work through this current set of challenges and for the financial markets to fully recover. In this environment, the economy will need a strong and stable financial system that can make credit available. We want banks to deploy capital and liquidity, but in a responsible way that avoids past mistakes and does not create new ones. The Federal Reserve is committed to working with other banking agencies and the Congress to promote the concurrent goals of fostering credit availability and a safe and sound banking system.

2010 UPDATE

On February 10, 2010, the Congressional Oversight Panel issued its report *Commercial Real Estate Losses and the Risk to Financial Stability*. This is a must read for anyone looking for more regarding this developing situation.

CHAPTER 5

Bailing Out a Sea of Debt

Sam Chandan, PhD, FRICS

Dr. Sam Chandan is President and Chief Economist of Real Estate Econo-metrics and an adjunct professor of real estate at The Wharton School of the University of Pennsylvania. In his leadership role at Real Estate Econo-metrics, Dr. Chandan is responsible for the firm's economic and risk analy-sis services, as well as its commercial mortgage performance reporting and forecasting products. Dr. Chandan is an Eminent Fellow of the Royal Insti-tution of Chartered Surveyors and the Vice Chair of RICS Americas' Eco-nomics and Capital Markets Council. In addition to the *Wall Street Journal*, Bloomberg, and Reuters, his commentary on the market has also appeared in the *Financial Times*, the *New York Times*, *Business Week*, and *Forbes*.

I am very appreciative of Dr. Chandan's contribution to this book. His reputation for accuracy in forecasting markets and depth of knowledge on this subject is well known throughout the United States.

COMMERCIAL REAL ESTATE MORTGAGE MARKETS AND POLICY INTERVENTIONS

By 2009, rising delinquency and default rates of multifamily and commer-cial mortgages had paved the way for the real estate sector's entry into the popular and policy discourse. From a barely discernible count of nonper-forming loans in early 2008, default rates for securitized mortgages climbed steeply as the credit crisis evolved and matured. The performance of bank-held loans has deteriorated as well, though the critical differences between portfolio and securitized (CMBS) mortgages have received little analytical attention.

The most visible policy interventions during 2009 focused on the com-mercial mortgage-backed securities (CMBS) market. The expansion of the

Term Asset-Backed Securities Loan Facility (TALF) to CMBS, announced in the spring of 2009 and implemented in June, was intended to trigger new activity in the otherwise dead securitization market. The further expansion of the TALF program to legacy CMBS was intended to enhance the liquidity of existing securities. And while the TALF program was warmly received when it was announced, as a practical matter, it did not do much to change the market's broader illiquidity in 2009. Instead, challenges facing banks in managing their commercial mortgage portfolios and reassessment of the risks and long-term role of agency financing have risen in prominence.

THE CMBS MARKET

To stem the rising tide of defaults of securitized commercial mortgages, the Treasury Department moved in the second half of 2009 to ease tax rules governing the modification of loans included in real estate mortgage investment conduits (REMICs). The policy change followed months of lobbying by the industry's representatives in Washington and was lauded as a significant step forward in the effort to contain the commercial mortgage debt crisis.

But how big a step was it? Until the adoption of the new rules, significant modifications to a securitization vehicle's loans risked triggering tax penalties except when "occasioned by default or a reasonably foreseeable default" [Treasury Regulations, Subchapter A, Section 1.860G-2(b)(3)(i)]. Under the complex tax rules, modified loans risked being treated as newly issued obligations that have been exchanged for the original, pre-modification obligations.

Until the 2009 changes were introduced, the prevailing view held that the possible tax consequences of Treasury regulation have limited interactions between strained borrowers and their servicers. Proponents of the new procedure contend that serious discussion of mortgage modification does not take place until too late because the Treasury's standard is not viewed as being met until "the loan is not performing or default is imminent."

The Internal Revenue Service's updated revenue procedure seeks to clarify the conditions under which the tax status of the structure will not be challenged (the new procedure appears in the October 5 Internal Revenue Bulletin No. 2009–40, pages 471–474). It also limits which loans will qualify for modification, principally as a function of value tests. Under the new regime, the servicer is held to a reasonable belief standard that there is a "significant" risk of default. To be sure, the reasonable belief "must be based on a diligent contemporaneous determination of that risk."

In an effort to encourage the proactive identification and management of problematic loans, the new procedure allows a determination to be made that the loan is at significant risk of default "even if the loan is performing"—in other words, before default occurs or is imminent. It would seem that borrowers and servicers are now free to negotiate modifications even if the problematic maturity is a way off, if the change substantially reduces the risk of default and if the fiduciary and economic justification obligations placed on the special servicer in the pooling and servicing agreement are fully satisfied. If a loan passes these tests, its servicer can then modify it in one or more different ways, including by changing the interest rate, writing down principal, extending amortization schedules, or other compromises. Such modifications may stave off an otherwise inevitable deterioration in mortgage performance.

In spite of the complex relationships and conflicting incentives of the stakeholders, these changes did remove a disincentive—whether real or perceived—for the revision of commercial mortgages otherwise at risk of default. By mitigating concerns about the potential *cost* of managing distress in securitized mortgage portfolios, this new policy presents the potential to improve outcomes for legacy CMBS. But the change is hardly a panacea for the commercial mortgage market. The new procedure fails to address the inevitable *moral hazard* and *scalability* problems that will arise. To the extent that it addresses and appears to resolve surface level concerns about the challenges facing the commercial mortgage marketplace without addressing the underlying structural and incentive issues that contributed to causing the problems, the new procedure and related efforts to support the CMBS market may ultimately prove counterproductive.

THE CASE OF PETER COOPER VILLAGE AND STUYVESANT TOWN

The seriousness of the CMBS market's challenges was underlined in late 2009 by the faltering of one of the industry's most notable transactions. The real estate industry was abuzz in late October following a New York State Court of Appeals' ruling in a lawsuit relating to rent increases at Peter Cooper Village and Stuyvesant Town. Under the luxury decontrol provisions of New York City's Rent Stabilization Law, former owner MetLife and current owner Tishman Speyer had raised rents on thousands of units in the massive 11,200-unit apartment complex. Upholding a lower court ruling from earlier this year, the appellate judges determined—though not unanimously—that the landlords should *not* have been able to raise rent-stabilized apartments to market rates while enjoying certain tax benefits for renovations of the complex.

The ruling was in stark contrast to the rating agencies' prior interpretations of the legal issues. In its early 2007 presale report for one of the related commercial mortgage-backed securities offerings, the rating agency assessed the situation as follows: "Counsels from both Tishman Speyer and MetLife have done extensive research on the J-51 tax abatement laws. Both parties are very confident that this lawsuit does not hold any merit, and the J-51 program does not in any way limit their ability to turn stabilized units into market rent units."

The presale report did not include any further assessment of the magnitude of risk should counsels' convictions prove to be misplaced.

If the new ruling survives appeal, the loss may prove very costly for the defendants. Under the relevant law, tenants may be entitled to treble damages on rent increases imposed in contravention of statute. If tenants are allowed to treat past years' overpayments as credit toward future rents, the property's cash flow could drop precipitously. The court dismissed claims by Tishman Speyer and MetLife that "predict dire financial consequences from our ruling, for themselves and the New York City real estate industry generally." Judge Read disagreed with his peers about this, however, stating:

> While it is true that dire predictions often prove to be mistaken, this is not always the case just because it usually is. After all, the Trojans would have done well to heed Cassandra. And you do not have to be gifted with her powers of prophecy to foresee significant, if not severe, dislocations in the New York City residential real estate industry as a result of today's decision. (Page 12 of the opinion.)

In Homer's *Iliad* and Lycophron's poem on the Trojans' unhappy fate, Cassandra receives the gift of prophecy from the god Apollo, who is beguiled by her beauty. Because she does not requite his love, however, Apollo adds a curse to his blessing: Notwithstanding her foresight, Cassandra's predictions will never be believed. She foresees the subterfuge of the Trojan horse, as well as the murder of mighty Agamemnon following his return to Greece from Troy. And yet she is unable to avert these tragic events.

The irony of invoking Cassandra's cursed gift may have escaped the dissenting justice. While the real estate industry's attention is now fixated on the potential for a default at Stuyvesant Town, this very outcome was suggested in 2006, when the sale of the property was first announced. But the market observers who derided the deal at the market's peak were treated as Cassandras in their own right. In late 2009, they would suggest that the apparent collapse of Tishman Speyer and BlackRock's $5.4 billion investment was easily foreseen and is altogether independent of the economy's having fallen into recession.

In late 2006, the property's cash flow was well below the debt service on the sum of the related $4.4 billion mortgage obligations. The loans were made under the premises that the property would be purchased for more than $480,000 per unit. In particular, it was assumed that cash flow would grow at a brisk pace as apartments were renovated or otherwise escaped rent stabilization. In the interim, an interest reserve of $400 million was set up to cover shortfalls in debt service coverage. Like the interest reserve, additional upfront reserves of $250 million—principally $190 million in a general reserve and $60 million in a capital expenditure reserve—are now almost totally depleted.

A rating agency reported in October 2009 that it was reviewing certain bonds related to the Stuyvesant Town loans. In an early 2007 presale report for the CMBS, that same rating agency used its estimate of calendar year 2011 cash flow to calculate its "actual" measure of Stuyvesant Town's debt service coverage. Employing a more pedestrian definition of "actual," the Stuyvesant Town's debt service coverage in late 2006 was approximately 0.4.

Apart from the specifics of the decision, a default of the magnitude and visibility of the Stuyvesant Town loans bears implications for a broader class of investors' perceptions of risk in holding CMBS exposure. Over the course of 2010 and beyond, such shocks may exert a chilling effect on current efforts to reignite securitization activity and liquidity in secondary CMBS markets. Confounding efforts to rebuild confidence in securitization, many investors in late 2009 viewed a default at Stuyvesant Town as a result of systemic issues in the CMBS market that have yet to be properly addressed, and not just as an asset-specific issue.*

BANK LENDING

The paralysis in the CMBS marketplace—except under the auspices of the Federal Reserve Bank and with the lubrication of low-cost credit—has exacerbated the challenges faced by bank lenders in managing their legacy portfolios. Efforts to reignite securitization while managing the consequences

---

*Following months of speculation that investors Tishman Speyer Properties and BlackRock Realty would default on mortgage obligations related to Peter Cooper Village and Stuyvesant Town, the sprawling apartment complex was turned over to creditors in the last week of January 2010. Unable to reach a compromise with lenders, Tishman and BlackRock gave up control of the property voluntarily to avoid a potential foreclosure. At the time of the transfer, market estimates of the property value fell in a range around $1.8 billion, one-third of the 2006 purchase price of $5.4 billion.

of its previous excesses will undoubtedly benefit traditional lenders as well. But that benefit is unlikely to be so far-reaching, at least in the near-term, that it will eliminate the need for direct and timely intervention in support of the keystone of sustainable, long-term credit availability.

With that in mind, and in the face of increasing pressure on banks to modify problematic commercial mortgages, the Federal Financial Institutions Examination Council (FFIEC)—which includes the Board of Governors of the Federal Reserve System, the Federal Deposit Insurance Corporation, the National Credit Union Administration, the Offices of the Comptroller of the Currency and of Thrift Supervision, and the FFIEC's own State Liaison Committee—released its anticipated "Policy Statement on Prudent Commercial Real Estate Loan Workouts" in October 2009. The new policy statement supersedes previous guidance used by examiners in evaluating the steps taken by banks in renewing and restructuring commercial mortgages. Encouraging prudent mortgage modifications, enhancing transparency in those modifications, and supporting the availability of credit to creditworthy borrowers are all among the stated goals of the FFIEC in releasing the new guidance.

In its policy statement, the FFIEC has indicated that banks that undertake prudent modifications of loan structures after thorough assessments of borrower conditions and capacities "will not be subject to criticism for engaging in these efforts." In a softening of the expected requirement that mortgage modifications should result in substantially lower default risks, the FFIEC absolved lenders of potential criticism "even if the restructured loans have weaknesses that result in adverse credit classifications." As for mortgages that are performing—on a current and prospective basis—and that have been made to high-credit-quality borrowers, the mere fact that the underlying real estate has dropped in value will not in itself trigger a mandatory and adverse reclassification of the mortgage.

The new guidance follows a series of material loss reviews by the Federal Deposit Insurance Corporation's (FDIC's) Office of Inspector General that have suggested a degree of laxity in the agency's oversight of commercial mortgage risks. The reviews, undertaken after bank failures, have cited rapid growth in acquisition, development, and construction financing and in commercial real estate exposures as causing the failure of some banks. Acknowledging conflicts of incentives within some banks, one recent review also cites "an incentive compensation program that paid a commission to a senior lending official based on the volume of loans and fees that the official originated." A number of the reviews describe how commercial real estate concentrations increased at specific lenders, and how the FDIC did not respond as vigorously as it might have.

And yet, this policy statement is not the first major regulatory foray into commercial real estate during the most recent cycle. In early 2006, a subset of the FFIEC agencies released proposed guidance, "Concentrations in Commercial Real Estate Lending and Sound Risk Management Practices," in response to how commercial real estate exposures on the balance sheets of many banks had increased. In the 11 months that passed before the final concentration guidance was promulgated, regulators and policymakers had to contend with a sometimes-visceral response to the perceived interference.

At the time, the market was enjoying a seemingly perfect alignment of rising fundamentals and even more rapidly rising prices and transaction volumes. During the comment period, a letter from one of the industry's leading associations stated that "the burden should be placed on the examining authority to demonstrate that the risk characteristics of a bank's commercial real estate portfolio warrant enhanced risk-management practices or increased capital." Following the promulgation of the final guidance, another leading association released a position statement, stating that it "objects to banking agency restrictions that unnecessarily constrain CRE lending."

The proposed concentration guidance elicited an unprecedented response from market participants. All told, the agencies received over 4,400 comment letters: "The vast majority of commenters expressed strong opposition to the proposed guidance and believe that the Agencies should address the issue of CRE concentration risk on a case-by-case basis as part of the examination process . . . Several commenters asserted that today's lending environment is significantly different than that of the late 1980s and early 1990s, when regulated financial institutions suffered losses from their real estate lending activities due to weak underwriting standards and risk management practices."

AGENCY FINANCING

The activities of bank and non-bank lenders during 2009 contrasted with the more direct interventions by the government through the channels of its newly acquired policy tools. More than one year after the Federal Housing Finance Administration (FHFA) and the Treasury Department's historic decision to bring these government-sponsored enterprises (GSEs) under the conservatorship of the FHFA, both institutions were struggling to return to profitability but were also keystones of credit availability for residential and multifamily markets in the United States.

Fannie Mae reported a third-quarter 2009 net loss of $18.9 billion, relating principally to $22 billion in credit expenses, up from a loss of $14.8 billion in the second quarter. Freddie Mac reported a relatively smaller net loss of $5 billion, including $7.6 billion in credit-related expenses. The latter's result was particularly revealing of current market conditions, however, since Freddie Mac had reported a relatively modest profit of $768 million in the second quarter of the year.

Under the terms of the senior preferred stock purchase agreement between the GSEs and the Treasury, the acting director of the FHFA made a request in November 2009 for funds necessary to offset Fannie Mae's net-worth deficit. To avoid a mandatory receivership under the terms of the Federal Housing Finance Regulatory Reform Act of 2008, the federal government will now transfer $15 billion to Fannie Mae. This transfer will bring Fannie Mae's net assets and obligations into balance for another quarter. Under the terms of the arrangement, the public commitment to Fannie Mae has risen to $60.9 billion over the past year. Freddie Mac, which maintained a positive net worth of $10.4 billion this quarter and which is not requesting additional Treasury funds for the time being, has received $51.7 billion to date.

To put the huge size of these financial commitments into context, note that at roughly $50.4 billion, Canada's entire federal budget deficit for 2009 ($54.2 billion in Canadian dollars) is smaller than the public transfers already made to either Fannie or Freddie. The support has come at a high cost to both Fannie and Freddie. Aside from their loss of independence, the dividend on the senior preferred stock is 10 percent. As a result, Fannie Mae now has an annualized dividend obligation of $6.1 billion payable to the Treasury; Freddie Mac, an annualized obligation of $5.2 billion. In its quarterly filing, Fannie Mae has indicated that its dividend commitment now exceeds its annual net income in five of the past seven years and that the expected growth in this obligation will make it increasingly difficult for Fannie Mae to return to profitability.

While many observable measures of housing market conditions were stabilizing in late 2009, Real Estate Econometrics projects that home foreclosures in 2010 will exceed 2009 levels. As of the third quarter, the serious delinquency rate for Fannie Mae's Single-Family Guaranty Book of Business had risen to 4.72 percent, up from 1.15 percent at the onset of the recession in the first quarter of 2008. The serious delinquency rate across Fannie Mae's Multifamily Guaranty Book of Business is 0.62 percent. The serious delinquency rate is highest for loans originated in 2007. The loss curve suggests that Fannie's 2008 multifamily mortgages will ultimately deteriorate further and faster than their 2007 counterparts.

The government lifeline to the GSEs, authorized up to a total of $400 billion at the crisis' apex, remained in place going into 2010. While the mechanisms of housing finance were still in need of a fundamental overhaul, the support system was warranted in light of the contribution of the GSEs to the housing recovery.

THE NEXT YEAR

With continuing challenges facing banks and other sources of credit in support of commercial real estate, evidence of commercial real estate as a focus of policy attention was increasingly visible at year-end 2009. Federal Open Market Committee (FOMC) minutes from late in the year, for example, singled out commercial real estate, noting that it was lagging behind broader economic trends: "In contrast to developments in the residential sector, commercial real estate activity continued to fall markedly in most districts, reflecting deteriorating fundamentals, including declining occupancy and rental rates, and very tight credit conditions."

The national default rate for commercial real estate mortgages held by depository institutions rose from 2.88 percent in the second quarter of 2009 to 3.40 percent in the third quarter, according to Real Estate Econometrics' analysis of data reported by regulated lenders and published by the FDIC. Over the same period, the multifamily mortgage default rate increased by 44 basis points (0.44 percentage points), rising from 3.14 percent to 3.58 percent. The principal contributors to the rise in the commercial and multifamily delinquency and default rates included (1) deterioration in property cash flow (from rising vacancy rates, falling asking and effective rents, and rising operating expense) resulting in an increase in the number of borrowers that were unable to meet current principal and interest obligations; (2) erosion of reserves available to cover shortfalls in debt service coverage; and (3) constraints on the availability of credit to support the refinancing of maturing mortgages. Mortgages originated in 2006 and 2007 are experiencing the most significant shortfalls in current cash flow relative to current debt service obligations. This is a result of the large number of mortgages underwritten to aggressively forecast prospective cash flow rather than to in-place cash flow during this period.

Despite the overall reported increase in the default rate generally, commercial mortgage performance varies dramatically across banks. The third quarter analysis shows that banks with similar concentrations in commercial real estate may have marked differences in delinquency and default rates. In particular, an analysis of loan performance at the 5,015 institutions with the largest exposures to commercial real estate shows *no* statistically significant relationship between concentration in real estate loans and default rate. In other words, the more detailed data shows little correlation between which banks had the worst problems and which are most exposed to real estate loans. The absence of a clear default rate-concentration relationship and variation in loan portfolio performance across institutions with similar concentrations reinforces that institutional factors, including risk management capabilities and accountability structures, may determine commercial

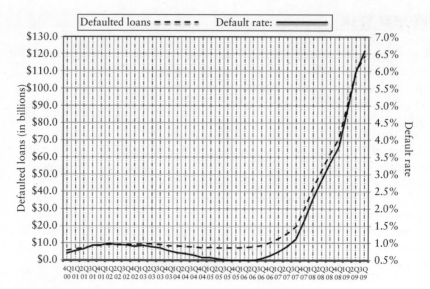

FIGURE 5.1   All Commercial Real Estate Loan Defaults
Source: Foresight Analytics LLC and subject to copyright.

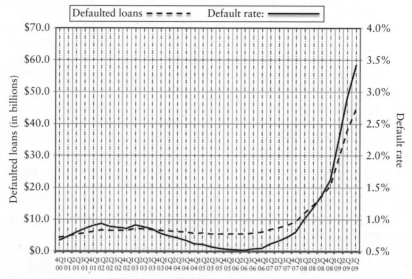

FIGURE 5.2   Commercial Mortgage Defaults
Source: Foresight Analytics LLC and subject to copyright.

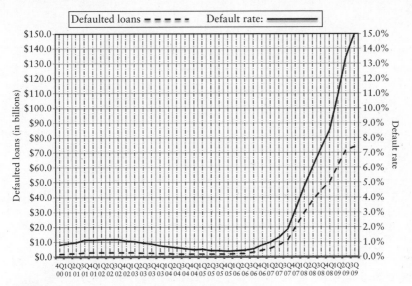

FIGURE 5.3 Construction and Land Loan Defaults
Source: Foresight Analytics LLC and subject to copyright

mortgage performance. General statements about the overall default rate (and reports based on undifferentiated data) frequently don't distinguish between various financial institutions.

Unlike the biggest banks, which have attracted a lot of public attention and headlines with their troubled complex finance activity, many well-managed American banks are doing much better than their competitors. These differences are easy to miss in the undifferentiated data frequently reported about financial institutions generally. As the headlines recede, the fundamental robustness in the balance sheets of a lot of small and medium-sized financial institutions will become clear, while others' weaknesses will become more apparent (see Figures 5.1 through 5.3).

Mitigation of Risks and Hazards: Survival Guide for Lenders, Owners, Buyers, and Commercial Real Estate Brokers

Lenders

Prepare for Impact

See no evil, hear no evil, and speak no evil." Remember those three mon-keys? "Extend and pretend," sound familiar? These approaches have become prevalent throughout the commercial lending industry today. As I've watched this wave approaching over the last year, I've personally managed a number of transactions involving distressed commercial prop-erties and observed the activities of the commercial lending institutions involved with these properties. Several of the transactions have been related to failed construction projects with outstanding loans. Many developers are unable to complete their construction projects, lease, sell, or refinance their projects once they are complete. Much of the problem is a reflection of the collapsing residential and commercial real estate markets due to the overall economic conditions.

The lack of available financing and the willingness of commercial lend-ers to lend is a major issue as well. Over the last year I have had clients with impeccable credit standing and significant net worth be denied the most rudimentary requests for refinancing or extensions of their existing loans. The banks' refusal to cooperate with these creditworthy borrowers, existing customers, and depositors have created loan defaults that otherwise could have been easily resolved and could have saved borrowers and lenders from the resulting losses.

WHEN THE WAVE HITS

My business partner, Gordon Stevenson, a 20-year veteran of commercial real estate, with an impeccable credit rating and substantial net worth, had a loan come due in early 2009. The loan was on a vacant commercial parcel located on a major signalized corner, just off the freeway and across from a well-known college. When Gordon purchased the property, he put 50 percent down and, due to the features previously mentioned, it was one of the few properties one could reasonably expect not to have fallen in value to any great extent. Unfortunately, loans on vacant land were difficult to get at the time, so months before his loan came due Gordon requested a temporary extension until suitable financing could be procured. He had never missed a payment and had a long-term relationship with the bank as well. The bank didn't hesitate—it went directly to threatening foreclosure if he didn't pay off the loan as agreed. Period. (I personally saw some of the 20 point font e-mails from the bank—the electronic equivalent to screaming their threats.) The bank made no effort nor offered suggestions for alternatives to the problem. It wasn't until after nine months of meetings, additional threatening e-mails, and total resistance by the bank, that Gordon finally hired an attorney. The bank was informed that foreclosure was an option being considered, and only then did the lender agree to what Gordon had asked for months before—a simple extension of the note until suitable financing could be obtained. What a waste of time, resources, and stress! That bank is now subject to a cease and desist order by the FDIC. This is not an effective way to manage issues with distressed loan situations, especially when it involves a credit worthy customer with a reasonable request for an extension. If that bank could extend the loan nine months after the request, it could have extended it when the request was made. This kind of poor decision making continues to this day by some banks despite the encouragement from government regulators to extend performing loans. This forces many otherwise creditworthy borrowers into foreclosures all over the country.

Many banks seem to be as lost as anyone else when it comes to knowing exactly what to do with the various situations presenting themselves in this difficult economy and in the battered commercial real estate markets.

Some of the commercial portfolio lenders have taken their loan officers, who underwrote most of the commercial loans now in default, and transformed them into "loan workout specialists" overnight. These newly ordained loan workout specialists are then assigned the duties of working out the issues related to the loans they personally underwrote. The conflicts are numerous and obvious. In many cases, the results have not been beneficial to anyone involved. A common stumbling block in this process is a tremendous delay in the acknowledgment that there is a problem with these loans to begin with.

Sometimes the "three monkeys'" impact on the lender's loan workout specialist's thinking is to the detriment of all concerned. For example: The borrower may say something like, "The condominiums are just not selling, and there are no prospects for the future." The lender's workout specialist may reply, "Can you make a payment next month?" never acknowledging what the borrower just said and the implications of that statement. Another common disconnect involves values:

Lender's Loan Workout Specialist: "Why don't you just refinance the property?"

Borrower: "It is only worth $10 million, and I owe you $15 million."

Lender's Loan Workout Specialist: "We have an appraisal from last year that says it's worth $10 million more than you owe."

I have been present for many of these types of conversations. Often, there was no inquiry on the part of the lender as to what the borrower was basing his statement on, no acknowledgment of a potential problem, and no serious effort to look closer at the situation. Just a passive reliance reference to the appraisal and "let's talk again next month." Intentional denial of the facts doesn't work. There are much better ways to address new factors in distressed loan situations as they come up in a way that will protect the lender's interests.

So it goes; many lenders at a loss as to what to do with an ever-expanding portfolio of nonperforming loans will often not address the obvious issue at hand. This can go on for months or even years in some cases. In many cases a notice of default will not be filed for a year or more while the property value and condition continues to decline. Conditions like those just described can lead to an asset being poorly managed; the borrower running out of money and options, and the lender losing the value of its asset. While commercial loan officers may have been very effective in their work as underwriters of commercial real estate loans, they are frequently struggling with the massive conflicts and challenges of their new jobs as loan workout specialists. Their lack of experience and training in handling special assets, foreclosures, and REOs (Real Estate Owned taken back by the lender in foreclosure), as well as conflicting regulatory issues result in further losses to the banks and lenders they work for. Lenders often struggle with the management of their special assets, addressing and resolving troubled loans, and how they ultimately will liquidate the property taken back in foreclosure. Depending on the borrower and the bank, as these situations increase and progress some existing procedures will not effectively protect any of the parties. Instead, they may result in greater losses to the lending institutions and potentially unnecessary damage to a borrower.

If a more realistic and effective strategy can be implemented from the very beginning, the end result will benefit all involved. Obtaining outside consultation from qualified advisors will assist in these matters and provide ideas for resolution outside the confines of a particular lender's culture or paradigm.

Recent surveys of thousands of lenders' distressed/special assets policies have revealed that certain proper management strategies applied to distressed loan situations (and the borrowers and properties related thereto) can lead to higher profitability for lenders who take the time to fully evaluate these matters on a one-on-one basis and then take appropriate action. Some lenders have radically changed how they process, manage, and resolve special assets matters to their own benefit and that of their borrowers.

In one case I was involved with, a newly constructed property had been vacant with no payments made for over one year and still no Notice of Default had been filed. The existing construction loan was in excess of $15 million. An offer of over $8 million was made to purchase the property; however, the existing lender opted to sell the note for millions less. In today's highly regulated environment, some banks must take these kinds of losses to satisfy regulatory pressures related to liquidity. However, in another case a building with an estimated $9 million loan (again over a year past due) was sold for around a third of the outstanding loan amount. If the bank had acknowledged the problem earlier and taken control of the property, it could've likely sold the building for twice what it ultimately received at a later date. This particular lender has now been taken over by the FDIC.

Lending institutions must prepare for this new wave of commercial real estate loan defaults and foreclosures. The holders of these defaulting commercial real estate notes (banks, thrifts, and other lending institutions), with foreclosures en masse, will ultimately become owners and managers of large commercial real estate portfolios over the next few years. This again represents a paradigm shift in the way commercial foreclosed properties have been viewed. Lenders have never had to handle so much responsibility for so much property at one time. The market conditions will likely force lenders to hold their newly repossessed real estate portfolios for extended periods of time, requiring better stewardship of their special assets. Not since the days of the RTC have we seen anything like this. A paradigm shift by definition requires new rules and new procedures; we must look forward not back.

Acknowledge the Problem

Before any productive action can be taken to prevent foreclosures, the problem must be acknowledged by both the lending institution and the borrower. I've designed strategies in concert with my lender clients designed to accumulate accurate data related to the subject property, and local/regional market conditions correlated to a borrower's ability to either sink or swim. A lender's strategy to get its arms around a troubled asset should include outside consultants who are qualified to give sound advice clear of any internal distractions.

With regards to values, market trend appraisals are not always the answer; in fact, many times they are a detriment to the situation. Appraisals, by design, look to history for their determinations of value. In a declining market as we expect to experience over the next several years, appraisals will not provide accurate estimations of "market" value unless appraisal standards are changed. I respect the good work of qualified appraisers; however, it must be acknowledged here that it is the commercial real estate brokers at large that provide the appraisers with their fundamental data, and it is the commercial real estate broker whom the appraiser relies on to confirm market data and valuations. Utilizing commercial broker price opinions and valuations with accurate investment analysis of the subject properties will be an important part of supporting a lender's objective. Commercial brokers can act as consultants supporting a lender in its assessments. Additionally, commercial brokers can help lenders and borrowers understand how serious the problem is and point to where the challenges are, plus any upside. This helps everyone make decisions designed to limit potential loses.

Commercial Loan Modifications

It seems inevitable that the commercial lending practices of the past will be replaced with similar procedures that assisted in the attempt to stabilize the residential real estate marketplace. Commercial loan modifications are occurring now. However, like the early loan modifications in the residential market, without an accurate strategy for designing modifications that offer the most promise for the borrower's and property's success, these early commercial loan modifications are likely to fail. Current failure estimates within the first three to six months are as high as 80 percent of the original loan modifications done in the residential sector. Therefore, it's important to have some kind of standardized approach and realistic commercial loan modification guidelines created to whatever extent possible. However, unlike the residential sector, in each commercial real estate transaction, borrower and property will bring a different set of variables. Any "standardized" approach will be limited by the nature of these transactions and will require a much more diligent and arduous process.

Some of this may take acts of Congress to implement. Regulatory agencies must be empowered to do what works to support the long-term health of the commercial real estate industry as a whole. Any standardized structure for commercial loan modifications must be done to have a lasting impact and help reduce the wave of commercial defaults we anticipate.

It's also important to acknowledge that the majority of the properties involved in this current transition may not qualify for commercial loan modifications due to their loss in value. Most properties will be detrimentally impacted by the reduction in values due to the falling rental rates, increases in vacancies, and, in the case of user properties, the owner's business being decimated by the economy. These properties inevitably must be taken back in the most cooperative way possible and resold at whatever price necessary. This can expedite clearing up these toxic assets, and begin to rehabilitate the commercial real estate sector as a whole. It would seem the small business administration (SBA) could play a role in this effort, not only with its own defaulting SBA loan portfolio but also by supporting new programs and assisting in the standardization of commercial loan modifications.

Accurate Assessments and Effective Property Management

Since many of these loans will likely proceed to default and foreclosure, it is more critical than ever that the lending institutions involved create procedures for the ownership, management, and ultimate disposition of these properties. The lender's new role as owner should be taken on in such a way that reflects the marketplace as a whole. If the financial institutions involved obtain early and accurate assessments of the properties by established and experienced commercial real estate brokers and property management companies, they will be protecting their assets and interests. Effective and accurate determination of actual condition, both physical and financial, and true market value must be done without the conflicts related to liquidity or balance sheet issues.

Lending institutions will fare far better if they adjust their approach to accepted market standards and limit the need for REO property sold at "fire sale" prices, instead of waiting too long or looking the other way, which only delays the inevitable. Incorrect valuation or old appraisal values applied to properties in default lead to unnecessary losses to the lenders involved. Special Assets departments should be involved from early on and have personnel trained in commercial real estate sales, escrow transaction, and property management. From the time the lender is notified of a borrower's problem or issues with the asset, the Special Assets department should intervene and stay involved. Lenders may want to consider the creation of new divisions or subdivisions of their Special Assets divisions, which could then become profit centers handling these assets while saving on service costs from outside contractors needed for sales and management.

The Special Asset divisions assigned to these properties should track them from start to finish. Commercial loan modification, consideration to asset management, and liquidation should be standardized to the extent possible so that the marketplace knows what to expect. This way more buyers and brokers may participate in the process of purchasing special assets as they become available. Commercial real estate lenders, as well as residential sector lenders, never made loans with the intent of becoming owners or property managers; they are neither structured to be owners, nor is it their purpose. Currently, lenders begrudgingly take these properties back, and once in their control, really struggle to manage and liquidate them as soon as possible. Many times, due to the lack of proper asset management, the properties' value deteriorates further. Outside contractors could help smaller lending institutions in these roles and the benefit of their expertise will likely pay for itself many times over if handled correctly.

Transforming from Lender to Owner

Just because the property is taken back in foreclosure doesn't mean that the responsibilities and duties of ownership should not be handled effectively. As previously mentioned in this section, damage is often done to the property's value due to a lender's lack of oversight in a default situation. Consideration of things as basic as property management, tenant satisfaction and retention, and maintenance must be kept in the forefront. When a prospective buyer purchases a property, it typically does an extensive analysis of the property, and evaluates the property's value potential and operating requirements. Lenders must do the same thing as they prepare to take properties back in foreclosure. Once taken back, the lender (now owner) must effectively operate a property with the same care and respect as an owner would. Ultimately, the lender/owner will be rewarded with higher values and respect in the marketplace.

When a seller prepares to sell a property, it typically gets multiple estimates of value from qualified marketing specialists, who know the property type and market area; lenders should do the same with their REOs. Some lenders will have the unfortunate burden of ownership of a large and diverse portfolio of REOs. Each REO will present different valuation and marketing challenges, and a lender should make sure its brokers are knowledgeable and experts with those particular challenges. With numerous properties in the lender's portfolio, discounts in fees may be available. Lenders should be cognizant of discounts available to them and exploit the competition for their business, remembering not to sacrifice quality of service for discounts in fees. With regards to commissions, fees, and property management costs, Special Asset divisions should have skilled personnel on staff assess the bank's position, as well as have the ability to accurately evaluate the market data provided by outside consultants and property managers.

It would be advisable to create standardized selling practices when a property is in the process of being sold on the open market. These practices should include processing incoming offers that are in line with what is typical in the marketplace. With all the lenders I have represented through the years, they rarely have the same process for selling their REOs as the general population of sellers. This detachment from the rest of the market can limit the pool of buyers for a lender's REOs and therefore limit the opportunity to attain the highest sales price possible.

In the commercial marketplace, if a second, higher offer comes in before the first offer is accepted, both offers would be considered. A seller's options include countering one or both of the offers. A lender/owner should know how to leverage offers to its benefit and do so as any other seller would using the standards and procedures recognized in the marketplace. Many lending institutions have opted to take an approach that is far less beneficial. In one case, an offer came in on a property, and we began negotiating on it. Then a second offer came in that was 20 percent higher and with superior terms to the first. In this case, the lender insisted on continuing to negotiate all the way through with the first offer in spite of the fact that another equally qualified, yet higher second offer came in prior to acceptance of the original. We ultimately went into contract with the first offer at a lower price. The first transaction failed to close and fortunately the second offer was still there. We went into escrow with the second offer and ultimately closed at the higher price. As lenders become owners, they will benefit from acting as an owner, behaving in a manner that suits the marketplace and encourages free negotiations and sales to the highest bidder (as opposed to back room deals).

SURVIVAL SKILLS—ERIC VON BERG, NEWMARK REALTY CAPITAL, INC.

I knew this section for lenders was critical given that the book's premise is based on the tremendous wave of commercial mortgage maturities set to occur over the next several years. I also knew I would have to reach beyond my own commercial real estate brokerage expertise to someone who lives and breathes commercial lending every day. So I turned to an established leader of the commercial mortgage banking industry, Eric Von Berg, CMB. Eric Von Berg is a well-respected leader in the field of Commercial Property Finance. He is a former chairman of the California Mortgage Bankers Association and sits on the Commercial Board of Governors (COMBOG) for the Mortgage Bankers Association of America. Eric is a principal at Newmark Realty Capital, Inc., in San Francisco, where he produces real estate mortgage and equity investments and consults in the areas of finance, asset management, and development. His company's activities as a commercial loan servicer give him insights that can benefit lenders and their industry greatly. What follows is my interview with Eric as we discuss the challenges and opportunities lenders have before them.

Tony Wood: First of all, let me start with asking you the question that I think a lot of people are asking and going to be asking: How did we get here in the first place? How did we end up with a trillion dollars of commercial debt, coming due in just the next few years and no way to refinance it? Is this the first time this has happened?

Eric Von Berg: Yes, it is, and I think it wouldn't be so disastrous if there was a source of funding to meet this need. Unfortunately, we totally transformed our funding system with the securitization industry, making other forms of lending obsolete, endangered, or extinct. Then, after converting everything to a different species, we killed it.

TW: When you say "we," what/whom do you mean?

EVB: The Fed and the states highly regulated the banks after the savings and loan crisis and basically eliminated the S&Ls, creating a capital scarcity in the late 1980s, early 1990s. Then, securitized lending, a new unregulated industry, blossomed into this highly regulated world to fill that gap. The regulations, mainly risk-based capital rules, that came out in the early 1990s hit the banks and also hit the large life companies and basically annihilated the S&Ls. These regulations forced the surviving banks to be cautious with their own funds and basically pushed them to become advocates in making money off this newfound way of doing things: Using other people's money and making loans off balance sheet, through securitized lending.

TW: So the emergence of CMBS was in a way created out of the free market clamoring for additional funding and ways to borrow and finding its way, one way or another. Sounds like the regulatory steps taken to restrain the commercial lending industry of the S&L era created new conduits for commercial lending and new ways for investors to capitalize on that demand.

EVB: Right: When you highly regulate something, you leave something on the side that is not regulated. It is just natural that everything is going to flow to the unregulated side.

TW: No matter how hard you try to regulate everything, it seems the market will find its way.

EVB: Yes. It will find the loophole, if there is one. And this was a big one.

TW: And was it a loophole? Was it a bad thing? That CMBS was created in itself?

EVB: No, it wasn't a bad thing. But it was this fiction . . . and the government relied on it . . . that the rating agencies were watching the store. And that really proved to be wrong.

That's what the residential sub-prime crisis did to commercial real estate; it killed securitization. I don't think we would even be having the commercial crisis; we wouldn't be having this 30 to 40 percent fall in the value of commercial real estate, if sub-prime hadn't killed securitization. Yes, commercial real estate values had gone too high, but they might have corrected 20 percent. We wouldn't be looking at them potentially being chopped in half.

TW: Which is what you anticipate in the next few years?
EVB: Yes, in many areas and sectors of commercial real estate values could fall 50 percent from the peak.

TW: Let's talk a bit about that. I can certainly see by the CoStar Statistics that I have been reading for many of the metropolitan markets throughout the nation that there is a consistently dramatic spike in vacancy factors and decline in rental rates across the board. Combine the loss in values with the continued economic crisis the entire country is experiencing and this huge wave of commercial debt maturity in the marketplace where there is practically no ability get a commercial real estate loan—that equates to me to even more downward pressures on values.
EVB: Absolutely. I'm taking apartments out of that because of "Fannie" and "Freddie." Basically, the government-sponsored agencies have taken over lending on multifamily, and as a result values are holding up much better in apartments. But, for other commercial property types today if the property has any issues, what we call "hair" on the deal, that deal may have to sell at its all-cash value because most buyers cannot get financing. There are so few "all-cash buyers," especially with the current market conditions; those few all-cash buyers have very high yield expectations. I'm working with a few and almost unanimously these buyers want to double their money in five years' time or less.

TW: And yet, the real impact of these conditions, that part of the cycle . . . doesn't seem to have hit just yet?
EVB: The wave is just beginning. Follow what's happened in subdivision land. In the beginning, the banks did not want to write their A&D loans and subdivision improvement loans down. They would extend and with each extension the regulations require the bank to get a new current appraisal.

For a long time the banks were able to get appraisals where everyone involved knew that the appraised value was way too high. But soon many subdivision properties were taken back and going on the market, and there were no buyers . . . and values fell over time to as low as 10 percent of the previous value in some cases. We are seeing finished lots begin to trade higher than they did at the absolute bottom in the spring of 2009. So maybe we can call the bottom on the residential cycle that started four years ago. By comparison, in commercial real estate, we are a year into this . . . or maybe 18 months of kick-the-can-down-the-road ignoring what's been happening. This "extend and pretend" can only happen because the appraisers are not saying, "Oh, it isn't a 7-cap rate, you know, it's a 10. And the rent the tenant is paying in the shopping center, you know, $4 per square foot per month, for a retail shop isn't market; it's $2." We are seeing this now in our softer markets . . . in Las Vegas and Phoenix, which are further down the curve.

Stronger markets aren't there yet, such as the San Francisco Bay Area. But in these weaker markets you can see strip malls selling at 14-caps. That's a 14-cap on the current rental income. If you drill down, though, it might be an 8-cap on current market rents.

TW: So, there are, in your opinion areas of the market place nationally that are certainly going to be hit worse than others?

Let's go down the list, in your mind, what do you think are going to be the worse areas hit? What are going to be some bright spots, if there are any?

EVB: The worst is probably going to be resort hotels and the high-end hotels. Here in San Francisco, The Stanford-Court has gone into default. The Four-Seasons has gone into default. The W Hotel sold for 50 percent . . . $220,000 per room, which is probably 40 percent under cost and less than half the value it would have sold for three years ago.

TW: I've talked to quite a number of people about this situation, and many people are not really aware of anything other than the CMBS issue. They don't realize that actually this trillion-dollar wave . . . the majority of it is holdings of mortgages by portfolio banks and thrifts. Unfortunately, given the mindset of the world today, when we talk of terms in trillions, it doesn't sound like a big number anymore.

EVB: The bank debt backlog of problem commercial real estate loans when you look at it in the light of small business credit drying up, such as the threat of CIT's bankruptcy—that's really scary stuff.

People keep talking about waves. The non-credit tenants in the buildings get their inventory and receivable funding and letters of credit for shipping goods from sources like CIT. You know, everybody is focused on the five big banks. The five big banks lend to state and local governments, hedge funds, the Fortune 500; but the major driver of our economy is small business, and when you start taking out small business lenders, then suddenly you have vacancies popping up, throughout commercial real estate, manufacturing disappearing, trade falling, unemployment shooting up . . . and then it becomes another wave that creates new lender problems that can lead to another tightening of credit, i.e., another wave, and so on.

TW: People keep talking about waves and tsunamis—the oceanic metaphors are really getting a lot of play these days. Right now, in the residential sector and that industry in California, Florida, and Arizona, they are talking about a third wave of residential foreclosures. In the commercial real estate industry we are talking about our "first wave," some people are calling it the great commercial real estate "bubble" or "the next shoe to drop."

There is a bit of mixing metaphors. . . . Have you heard about the "eight bubbles"? Some are talking about the "eight bubbles" and in that conversation, this is the first of eight to pop! So, bubbles, waves, balloons popping, shoes falling . . . it's all quite interesting. It's clearly our attempt to get our arms around what we are dealing with.

So, what is a lender to do? What I'm finding . . . and you already reiterated this a bit . . . lenders' entire mindset is still broadly based in historical data and historical behavior and policies . . . and in some ways guided by regulatory restraints.

EVB: Correct.

TW: Would you agree that lenders are going to have to recognize the paradigm shift within their own industry and start looking outside the box to manage what is likely to be a historic repossession of assets and preparing to own a huge amount of real estate?

EVB: Yes. But, there are things they *can* do. If they become more responsible managers, looking at the operation of the real estate asset, like you suggest, versus their normal servicing response. Common sense and a focus on the real estate value fundamentals will help these lenders not take as many properties back. Today is different than the early 1990s, not all problem commercial loans are situations where the value of the property has fallen below the loan amount. We are facing a lot of situations where you have a conservative borrower with plenty of equity in the property above the loan, where he is facing a default because he can't get the lines of credit he needs anymore to operate his property portfolio. For example, the borrower needs to get funding to build the T.I.'s on a half-leased property when he has a new tenant in tow. I have seen this situation; the owner has 50 percent equity in the property and can't get a T.I. loan or even a line of credit anywhere. This is a well-qualified investor, the kind of guy who has a $3 million house and always keeps it with a low mortgage so he can pledge it to the bank to get a line of credit. He can't find that gap financing today anywhere.

We have a choking off of credit that will have lots and lots of ramifications. In this same case the borrower goes to his existing lender, the loan is $20 million, his equity is $20 million, and he needs $2 million to put in the new tenant. There is room for it. There will be plenty of cash flow and debt coverage once the new tenant occupies. Give him the $2 million! The existing lender says, "No, we're worried about this loan because of the vacancy. Also our hands are tied: We are not going to mess with this loan because the regulations would call the increased loan a workout and require us to multiply the amount of equity—our risked based capital—we have to post against this loan. So—get the funds somewhere else."

These kinds of situations will start to absolutely clog the bankruptcy courts. It's a new paradigm: The borrower's lawyer will go to the judge and say "The property is not upside down, there is plenty of equity: Bankruptcy court, screw that lender, save this guy's hide because it's not his fault; he did nothing wrong. It's the world financial markets. Otherwise, the borrower's equity will be unfairly wiped out." I am convinced, we haven't seen it yet, that a number of bankruptcy judges will say, "You're right." Let's just tie that lender's hands for five years or whatever . . . until the market comes back for lending. It could get really weird.

TW: As the wave hits and we are pushed toward that capitulation phase, people will start talking about it and clamoring for assistance. Unfortunately, we don't have quite the political weight of a primary residence homeowner; someone who is living in it. This is business property. These are investments. There is a real trend to let investors and lenders involved take their hits . . . and if it goes back into foreclosure, and diminishes in value . . . by 40 to 50 percent or more, oh well, that was the risk they took. Let's move on. Obviously, banks are going to be taking a lot back. The question is how much? It's going to be historic in size and volume. Do you agree that the amount is going to be historic in nature?

EVB: Yes, it is. It's going to be historic. However, the new market for selling discounted notes will make it look a lot less severe. [. . .] The lenders actually will take the losses, but they won't show a lot of REO.

TW: Let's talk about the selling of these notes. It's not just the selling discounted notes, but the methodology and manipulation of the marketplace involved that has my attention. It is like a new emerging marketplace this trading in the buying and selling of these discounted notes.

You have individuals seeking out tranches of loans, sometimes ones they have a personal interest in for one reason or another and systematically making huge profits overnight. For example, consider a million dollar loan on a $2 million property in a tranche of troubled assets. During the buyer's "due diligence" he contacts the borrower says, "Hey, how would you like a 30 percent reduction to refinance your loan?" If you can refinance it, we'll give it to you." This is the "due diligence." The guy says sure, he can do it for a 30 percent principal reduction on his note. The buyer buys the note at 30 cents on the dollar; the borrower refinances to pay them off at 70 cents on the dollar; everyone is happy. This is causing a huge downward pressure in the marketplace and simply because the lenders need to liquidate these notes due to regulatory pressures. It's a vicious, damaging cycle.

EVB: The regulatory issues with the banks are causing this. The restrictions on workouts and discounted payoffs by borrowers are why you see this sort of cottage industry of note buyers emerging. The game plan for these note buyers is to cut the deal with the borrower the lender can't make and turn the note buyer's money, as quickly as possible and make a quick pop.

TW: But what it did is further diminish value of the bank, its notes, and property values. The bank left a lot on the table. It could have gone directly to the borrower and offered the same principal reduction and made much more than selling the note. The banks could create standardized programs to offer these discounts to borrowers of their choosing. Why give this away to outside investors?

EVB: Yes, and what is interesting is that the CMBS world doesn't have the same regulations as the banks and life insurance lenders. So, regulatorily speaking, the CMBS special servicer can cut a deal with the borrower if a discounted payoff is in the best interest of the CMBS investors. In the bank and life insurance worlds, they are severely penalized for giving borrowers a discounted pay off—a DPO.

TW: If the banks are already taking upwards of 70 percent losses on these notes, classified as "special assets," "troubled assets," whatever you categorize them as, to cash buyers, can't the regulatory issues be addressed to offer the same discount to the borrowers themselves? Isn't this what they have done in the residential sector permitting principal reductions and modifications of the loans? I know at this time by regulations it is not permitted; however, wouldn't it make sense to allow the holders of these notes, the lenders, banks, and thrifts to do it for themselves?

EVB: Yes, when you assume all players are honest, it looks like a lot of logic got lost when they regulated the banks and insurance companies after the last commercial real estate debacle. But remember, after digging into the S&L crisis, regulators found a lot of self-dealings in the world of S&Ls. They lent to their buddies . . . and to themselves. These crooked S&Ls cut favorable deals with their friends, including deep "discounted payoffs." If encouraged by new regulation, DPOs could again be a really abused thing.

Clearly new regulation is on the way. A new crisis can result from the loopholes and regulations Congress wants to come up with as a response to our current problems. When a loophole is created no one knows its ultimate effect. It is like Adam saying to Eve after a bite of the apple, "Stand back, we don't know how big this is going to get."

Some changes are needed because the "REMIC Rules" that affect CMBS lending are the same REMIC Rules that affect residential RMBS. For example, REMIC rules do not allow carry-back financing on the sale of REO. REMIC reform is needed, but you have some Congress people trying to force the servicer's hand to give generous deals to borrowers. Makes sense; more borrowers vote than lenders. These congressmen have a lot of foreclosures in their home states and are pushing "REMIC Reform," at least in the eyes of the Mortgage Bankers Association, in the wrong direction. If the CMBS bondholders are hurt because the rules change on them midstream, these investors may never come back to securitized lending. We will see where this all comes out.

TW: What are your thoughts on commercial REOs, banks, taking back commercial properties resulting from their defaulting loans, and how they handle the process now versus how they should handle these situations? What kind of changes do you think need to be made?

EVB: I can tell you from a commercial real estate industry standpoint: I'm always surprised at such a well-educated, analytical type of industry and people that work within it are very prudent . . . yet they can for some reason be unwilling to consider pragmatic methodologies. They should incorporate asset management methodologies that are used in the commercial real estate industry as a whole . . . and apply them to their commercial REOs. Many institutions leave lots of money on the table. Though misguided REO practices are not universal; I think some companies do a better job with REOs then some of the others.

Because of "the hair on the deal that you can't see until you own it," there certainly should be a discount on the resale of commercial REOs. However, the process in the way the lenders take these properties back, the delays involved there, can be damaging to their own interests. Then, after they take control of the property, the way they sell it does not reflect some very standardized policies that people outside the banking industry, typical owners/operators of commercial real estate do to protect their investments and to get the highest dollar.

If it turns into a year process . . . then eventually the property sells exactly at the number that I could have gotten an offer for, the day it went bad, the lender has lost out.

TW: As you look at the commercial real estate markets for 2010, what areas are you most concerned about and what changes (regulatory or otherwise) will be helpful to the situation?

EVB: Tony, I think the current optimism by the press and politicians about the economy having hit bottom is overblown. We experienced a collapse of an asset bubble not unlike that of Japan's in the late 1980s. I hope we do not take as long to recover as Japan, but the recovery will not be swift. For 20 years, our government, our corporations, and the public hyped consumption based upon cheep credit from overseas.

The World War II generation grew up in the depression and did not believe in debt. They invested in infrastructure and assets that were left to us largely unleveraged. We mortgaged these assets—our homes, our businesses, and our government—to the hilt to support a lifestyle beyond a level justified by our own rate of savings and taxation. For two decades we floored an eight-cylinder engine but only had gas for six cylinders—so we borrowed the rest. It is going to be slow going for awhile.

Over the last couple months we have seen a near equilibrium of layoffs and job formation. This balance would slump back into massive job losses if the effect of the various stimulus measures and tax cuts were eliminated. Many of these measures are scheduled to expire in 2010. Interest rates are artificially low. Our government is giving tax credits to home buyers and then either guaranteeing or outright buying the mortgage backed bonds—to the tune of 80 percent or more of all new home mortgages. This cannot continue.

The commercial real estate market was largely responsible for the country's economic downturn in the late 1980s early 1990s Almost on our own, we pulled the country down then and we are about to do it again. This impending commercial real estate debacle could coincide with tax cuts expiring and government stimulus being largely spent. The CRE debacle will also coincide with what I call the impending exhaustion of private reserves. Economists have not focused on the fact that many people and small business are surviving on the remnants of savings and 401(k) investments. It is okay for people to live for a few months or even a couple years dipping into reserves. But we are approaching a time when these private reserves are exhausted.

The areas of commercial real estate that will be hurt the hardest are those whose tenants are small businesses where these businesses do not have access to the capital markets and must rely on community banks for lending. I am talking about strip retail, distribution, small tenant light industrial, and office properties. Especially hard hit will be buildings with three or fewer tenants. Lenders today are avoiding what they call "binary risk." A single tenant goes out and the property suddenly cannot make the debt service payments. These properties are almost unfinanceable.

Newmark Realty Capital, Inc. is active in two emerging areas that will get a lot of attention in the next 24 months. One is debt advisory: We are working with borrowers whose properties are worth substantially less than the loan amounts to craft solutions that leave borrower and lender in a better place than a foreclosure. The second area, believe it or not, is securitized lending: Yes, there are the beginnings of CMBS coming back. It is looking a lot like the early days of CMBS. Underwriting is conservative; rates are higher than portfolio lenders, and better reflect the risks involved. But it is nonrecourse lending on assets passed over by the banks and life companies. Our life insurance lenders are great, but they only had about a 10 percent market share—so the need for replacement financing is great.

CMBS Loan Modification Question and Answer and Motivations of the Special Servicer

Provided by Eric Von Berg, Newmark Realty Capital, Inc.

Q: What governs the modification process for a conduit (CMBS) loan?
A: The important document is the Pooling and Servicing Agreement (PSA) for the REMIC trust, as well as the REMIC tax laws.

Q: Can CMBS loans be modified?
A: Yes. Previously it was only possible as long as the loan was not in default and only nonmaterial modifications were allowed. However, once the loan was moved to Special Servicing, most normal loan modifications were allowed. Recent changes also allow for earlier workouts as well.

Q: What modifications aren't allowed?
A: The REMIC trust is not allowed to advance more money, sell performing loans, make a new loan, and many PSAs limit the extention of loans beyond two years.

Q: How do I get my loan moved from the Master to the Special Servicer?
A: Usually, the loan needs to be 90 days delinquent. However, your mortgage banker or attorney may be able to advise you on how to appeal an "imminent default" to the Special Servicer to get your loan transferred without a delinquency.

Q: Why would a Special Servicer modify or extend a loan?
A: The sole criterion used by the Special Servicer is what maximizes the return to all the CMBS bondholders. The best interest of the borrower is not important.

Q: How does a Special Servicer determine if a proposed modification, discounted payoff (DPO), or extension is in the best interest of the bondholders?
A: They are required by the Pooling and Servicing Agreement to use a net present value (NPV) calculation to measure all alternatives. The base case is what the REMIC trust would recover in foreclosure.

Q: Should I attempt this on my own?

A: Generally not. You should use a mortgage banker and attorney who are active in the world of CMBS servicing and who know the motivators and constraints on the Special Servicer. Your consultant should know how to prepare the case, giving the Special Servicer the documentation and the justification needed to make the desired decision.

MOTIVATIONS OF THE SPECIAL SERVICER

- **Money:** The Special Servicer gets a servicing fee but also keeps 100 percent of default interest and extension, modification fees. It gets a 1 percent disposition fee on foreclosure.
- **Close Relationships:** The Special Servicer is usually owned by the holder of the first loss position, i.e., the B-piece or unrated tranche.
- **Workload:** The more your mortgage banker can do to lighten the workload of the Special Servicer, the better.
- **Cover:** Documented justification needs to be in the Special Servicer's file for all decisions that are made. See the previous Q&A section. An important measure—preserving the value of the real estate asset.
- **Civility:** Jerks are targets for foreclosure. Ask nicely: You have little leverage. The reputations of the hired consultants help. They have done this before. They know what is negotiable and what is not.
- **Controlling Class:** The control of the REMIC can shift from the initial holder of the first loss position to more senior bondholders. Today the A classes want solutions that get to cash fast: DPOs, note sales, or foreclosures.

COMMERCIAL LOAN WORKOUTS FROM THE LENDER'S PERSPECTIVE—MAURA O'CONNOR, SEYFARTH SHAW LLP

As discussed in the chapter on workouts from the borrower's perspective, the real estate lawyers in our firm's nationwide distressed assets team are seeing increasing defaults and resulting workout and foreclosure activity. As noted, many distressed loans that result in foreclosures could have been worked out, if certain simple and seemingly obvious steps were taken by both the lender and borrower/developer to cooperatively work out a consensual resolution. At the risk of stating the obvious, here's a brief overview of issues that lenders need to consider in working out problem loans. While some of these points should be obvious to experienced lenders, it's always a good idea in a workout to return to the basics, to check each of the usual elements of a possible resolution for holes and issues.

Lender Mindset

Unsurprisingly, lenders want to get their loans repaid. Their mindset is, "You borrowed the money and said you'd repay it; now it's time to pay it or surrender the collateral." But most lenders don't really want to take over the development or management of the financed real estate. They typically don't have the skills needed to develop, lease up, or manage property, nor do they want the liability of an active developer (especially if the lender is an institution). Lenders also know that if they foreclose, rather than doing a workout, they probably will recover less—especially if the foreclosure is contested or the borrower files for bankruptcy.

If a workout or extension is done early enough, some types of lenders may be able to avoid having to reclassify the loan as a bad loan, which often costs them extra, as they must reserve additional capital against the potential loss. (Whether the lender is a portfolio lender, who originated and holds its own loan, or a CMBS lender, where the originator sold off all or most of the interests in the loan, and the loan is being serviced by a servicer, may to a large extent determine the flexibility the lender has to modify the loan.) However, while most lenders would rather complete a consensual workout than a foreclosure, they typically don't want to loan more money into a troubled project, unless they can see a clear exit that will result in a full repayment of the loan.

So, if they can see a reasonable plan for doing so and have enough flexibility from their internal management and external regulators or investors, many lenders usually would rather extend or modify their loans than foreclose on the collateral for them. This can leave the borrower/developer in charge, operating the property, as long as there is some realistic possibility of a repayment over time.

Most lenders will typically assess fairly early on whether a distressed loan can be repaid in a reasonable time and what the current value of the project is. If the project is not salvageable, the lender typically will foreclose on and sell the collateral to collect as much of the outstanding amount as possible. In deciding whether to negotiate a workout or to foreclose, many lenders assess whether a borrower falls one of two informal categories: first, the borrowers that are straightforward about the project and that add hard-to-replace value to the collateral (for example, by working hard to increase the project's income, or by providing more equity or more collateral); or, second, borrowers that are not likely to add value or are not playing straight with their lender. In the current market, lenders' distressed loan departments are often overworked and understaffed; so these "good or bad" decisions sometimes will be made quickly and cursorily, not after careful study. In seeking a workout in a downturn, *first impressions count*. A borrower that falls into the "bad" category will typically not be able to negotiate a workout—the lender's representative will make triage decisions to spend time negotiating only the workouts that are likely to lead to a deal. Obviously, there are costs associated with a foreclosure, which may become very expensive if the borrower opposes it or files for bankruptcy protection. The prudent lender will carefully consider the borrower's behavior in analyzing whether it makes sense to spend the time and resources to attempt a workout of a troubled loan.

If it is willing to do a workout, a lender typically must accomplish four goals: It must (1) improve the lender's legal rights and remedies if the borrower ultimately defaults on the restructured loan; (2) preserve or enhance its collateral for the loan (and many lenders simply won't do a workout unless the borrower will bring in new equity); (3) avoid worsening its legal position by giving the borrower claims and defenses that the borrower does not currently have; and (4) implement changes to the payment, collateral, or other terms of the loan to make it more likely that the lender will ultimately collect more than it would otherwise collect at foreclosure.

Lender Leverage

Once a borrower defaults or is in danger of defaulting on its loan, the lender has more leverage: If the borrower won't or can't pay back the loan, the lender can and will foreclose on the project. And there is usually no obligation on the part of a lender to work out a loan. Again, at the risk of stating the obvious, if the borrower does not repay the money it borrowed, the lender typically has the right to enforce its loan documents by foreclosing on the collateral and may also have the right to pursue additional repayments from borrowers or guarantors. This may be done in different ways depending on the state where the property is located, but ultimately this is the lender's big stick.

Often the lender and borrower cannot agree whether there would be any real value (equity) left in the property after repayment of the loan. If the lender and borrower both know there will be no equity left after repayment, neither side has much incentive to instead do a workout unless the borrower is willing or able to put in more money in hopes of realizing a long-term gain on the property. (Or unless the lender does not want to take the property back, for some reason, like a property that is severely environmentally contaminated.) However, if the lender and borrower do not agree whether there's equity remaining in the property, then one side or the other will be motivated to work out the deal if possible—and the other, less motivated.

The lender may have the right to go after the borrower's other assets, or those of a guarantor. This is the lender's second biggest stick. Or maybe this is the biggest, if the borrower has significant other assets or the guarantor is an attractive collection target. While most lenders don't want to wipe out a reputable borrower or guarantor who has been a good customer in the past and is facing difficulties now, they want to get repaid. (One lender told me that, while he did not want to wipe borrowers out, he had no qualms about repayment of a loan that would require a borrower to scale back his standard of living. In my experience primarily working as lender's counsel, that's pretty typical.)

In fact, a lender's representatives owe a duty to its investors and shareholders to collect as much as possible on the loan and any guaranties. While most if not all lenders are generally reasonable if the borrower plays fair and is doing its best, some borrower tactics are not welcome. If the borrower or guarantor starts playing games, such as hiding information or lying, taking money generated by the property to pay other debts, or opposing foreclosure where there's no or little equity in the property, the lender will be more likely to aggressively press forward with enforcing the loan against all available assets of the borrower and any guarantors.

Obviously, there's a cost to enforcing a loan; depending on the difficulty under the applicable state law of collecting on a particular asset, a lender may elect not to bother going after that asset. For example, in California, a lender may not pursue any other judicial cause of action, such as suing the borrower directly, without foreclosing on the real property collateral. But such a lender usually may start either or both of a nonjudicial foreclosure sale (aka a trustee's sale), which takes less time and is cheaper, and cuts off the borrower's redemption rights . . . or a more formal judicial foreclosure proceeding, which takes a lot longer, is a lot more expensive, and allows the lender to seek a "deficiency"—the amount still owed in excess of the purchase price for the property paid at the nonjudicial foreclosure sale—against the borrower, but gives the borrower redemption rights for up to a year. To decide which way it wants to enforce the California loan, a lender and its counsel must figure out:

- What the real estate collateral (and any other collateral) is worth.
- Whether the loan is of a type where getting a deficiency is allowed.
- If the borrower has other assets available to satisfy a deficiency.
- If a guarantor has assets available to repay the loan or a deficiency, and several other issues.

This typically takes some time and effort, because a wrong move can seriously impair, or even cut off, the lender's rights to its collateral. In some other states, where the lender can elect to sue the borrower directly, a lender may do so instead of foreclosing on the real property first, especially in a down market if the property is worth less than the debt but the borrower has significant assets.

Legal Review: The Lender Should Know What Its Documents Say

Just like the borrower, the lender should hire new counsel to review its loan documents. The point of bringing in a fresh set of eyes is that lawyers, like other humans, tend to see what they expect to see. A lawyer who negotiated a deal may not see the flaws in the documents (and has an incentive to avoid disclosing any such flaws to the lender client). The lender usually has enough money to hire good counsel. If competent and experienced local counsel is hired, she or he should be able to find any flaws in the documents. Then, if a workout or extension is done, the lender can typically fix any loan documentation problems as part of that deal.

While it may sound like I'm harping on the problems in loan documents, it's surprising how often loan documents, particularly those done in the late stages of a boom, contain very serious errors. And courts will penalize errors for documentation flaws. Some years ago, I successfully foreclosed on a loan (not documented by my firm) where the legal description of the property was seriously incorrect. That foreclosure was touch and go: We only prevailed after having to bring in a litigator and arguing for months through a judicial foreclosure for reformation of the legal description, making a motion *nunc pro tunc*. That's translated loosely as "Please, your honor, we gave them the money—put it back the way it should have been! And please let us take the collateral back." I can't possibly overstate how many loan documents include typos in names, amounts, or other key parts of the loan documents, primarily because no one bothered to do the work properly the first time (or perhaps because no one wanted to pay for the work to be done properly, because that person did not anticipate any possible collection problems). Since many foreclosure laws are persnickety exercises in form over substance, those little mistakes can kill a lender's rights to collect the collateral stone dead. Bottom line: Hire lawyers who can, and do, proof their work.

To guard against some of the most obvious documentation and origination mistakes, here are some things a lender and its counsel should check up front when considering a loan modification, workout, or foreclosure. Any request from a borrower for an extension or other modification provides an opportunity for a forward-thinking lender to confirm that its documents are in good shape so that if the borrower ultimately cannot or will not pay the loan, the lender can foreclose—or to fix them if the documents contain errors—long before a more serious default occurs or foreclosure is imminent:

- Review all loan documents without reading any summaries first (so you see what's actually written on the controlling documents).
- Note any changes from the lender's standard provisions (such as extended cure or notice periods).
- Ask whether any changes have been allowed but have not been documented, or whether lender has entered into any other agreements with borrower parties, or has taken any other actions with respect to borrower parties, which might give rise to lender liability.
- Check for common defects/deficiencies, such as incorrectly identified parties, lack of or incomplete suretyship waivers, incorrect collateral descriptions and UCC financing statements, defective cash management agreements, missing or unattached allonges if the note has been modified, undated or not fully executed documents, missing exhibits, unfinished post-closing items, missing title insurance policy, missing original note.
- Confirm the real estate collateral is correctly described and matches the survey.
- Check to see if any Subordination, Non-disturbance, and Attornment Agreements have been signed by major tenants, or should have been.
- Confirm that all needed consents for personal property collateral were obtained, that all descriptions of that collateral are complete and correct, and that all steps necessary to perfect and preserve the lender's security interest have been taken.
- Review status and priority of advances over mechanics' liens.
- Review evidence of environmental condition of property.
- Investigate any changed circumstances of the borrower, guarantor, or property or ownership of the collateral.
- Analyze the applicability of any changes in the law.
- Confirm that lender actually has in its possession all needed original documents.
- Check to determine whether all post-loan closing items have been finished.
- Review updated title information to determine if any new title issues or claims have arisen since the loan was funded.
- Conduct and review updated searches of UCC, tax, and judgment liens concerning borrower and any guarantor.
- Check to see if any circumstances have changed (such as the borrower's name or jurisdiction of organization) and investigate any other issues relevant to the particular borrower, loan or property.

Business Review: The Lender Usually Knows What the Property Is Worth (or Can Find Out)

The lender will typically hire an appraiser to evaluate the property, and the value will guide the lender's business and strategic enforcement and workout decisions. A good appraiser, who is competent to testify in court if needed, is absolutely vital. It is not uncommon for workout and even bankruptcy outcomes to be determined utterly by a dispute over the actual value of the underlying real estate. So don't go into that possible battle unarmed.

Frequently, lenders may not have as much knowledge about the potential upside of, or challenges facing, a given property as the developer/owner, so the developer/owner may be able to provide the lender with more information to build on the lender's appraisal of the property, which may lead to more creative resolutions of the outstanding loan.

In addition to reviewing an updated appraisal, a lender should obtain and review borrower's and any guarantor's updated financial statements, the actual use made of the loan to date, project budgets, borrower's compliance with loan covenants including financial covenants, market conditions, borrower's and guarantor's ability to pay, and other criteria used by the lender to determine if a workout is feasible and would net the lender a better return than would a foreclosure.

Lender's Early Stage Moves

Once a lender decides to negotiate a possible workout of a real estate loan, there are several steps it usually will take.

- A lender will probably require that the borrower enter into a *"pre-negotiation" agreement*: an agreement to limit any claims by the borrower that it relied on statements by the lender or its representatives when negotiating a potential workout. These agreements usually expressly stipulate that any discussions between the parties are settlement discussions and won't be admitted as evidence in any later litigation between the parties. This agreement is very important to preserve the lender's right not to enter into a workout at all, or on terms that the lender finds unacceptable. These agreements typically provide, among other things, that there is no legally binding agreement to modify the loan until and unless it is fully documented in a writing signed by all parties. They also usually include a requirement that all of the lender's costs be paid up front by borrower and/or any guarantors.
- A lender may elect to *transfer the loan* to a separate newly formed special purpose entity. This allows the lender to shield itself from potential

new lender liability claims arising as a result of any workout, workout negotiations, or foreclosure activities.

- A lender may take steps to put pressure on the borrower and/or to *gain control of the property by initiating foreclosure proceedings* (under real estate law and/or under the Uniform Commercial Code), *seeking appointment of a receiver, exercising its right to collect rents*, or taking any other enforcement steps. This is frequently done to speed up the process of figuring out whether a workout is possible, while starting the clock running on foreclosure for the lender. Lenders frequently take one or more of these steps for one of three reasons: (1) many attempted workouts cannot be successfully negotiated, so the loan ultimately is foreclosed anyway; (2) many borrowers wait until they are defaulting or about to default before contacting their lenders to attempt to work out a loan; and (3) many borrowers frequently do not bring realistic expectations and/or meaningful concessions to early stage workout negotiations, instead dragging them on. In particular, we have seen many borrowers who could sell some of their equity interests to raise cash refuse to do so because they don't like the offered price, apparently forgetting the risk that they could be foreclosed if they don't work out a resolution. A lender is more likely to do a deal with its borrower if the borrower acts cooperatively and is willing to "cut to the chase," even if that means making painful concessions.

- If it thinks a borrower is acting in good faith and is acting rationally, a lender may enter into a *short-term forbearance agreement* to refrain from exercising its remedies for a specific short period of time to give the borrower and lender time to work out a deal. These agreements range from simple, with few conditions, to extensively negotiated, and can impose many more obligations on borrower. If there are deficiencies in the loan documents, it is often prudent for a lender to condition its entering into a forbearance agreement on borrower's execution and delivery of documents that fix any such problems.

Negotiating the Workout

Based on its business and legal reviews concerning the loan, and any additional information provided by the borrower, the lender and its counsel will negotiate a workout. Typically, the parties work off one or more non-enforceable terms sheets that set out the basic terms and conditions. Usually, the basic framework of the workout deal is based on ideas proposed by the borrower. Many lenders are concerned that if they make the first offer of workout terms, and it does not work out, the borrower may later claim that the project failed because the lender overstepped its appropriate boundaries by telling the borrower what to do. Regardless of who makes the first offer, however, many issues need to be addressed, including the changes in timing and amount to the payment terms of the loan; the possible addition of supplemental collateral or guaranties; tax issues affecting borrower and lender (note that both portfolio lenders and special servicers administering CMBS loans usually face tax consequences from modifications of loans). If the loan did not already impose a lockbox or other cash management arrangement on borrower, a lender frequently will seek to impose one so that it can control the cash generated by the property as the property's tenants pay rents.

Documenting and Closing the Workout

When the basic terms are settled, the workout must be documented. Frequently, additional issues arise at this point; sometimes they can be resolved, sometimes not. Loan workout documents frequently include the basic terms of the deal modifying the loan; covenants by borrower parties to do certain things (pay reduced amounts, meet certain financial standards, and the like); acknowledgments, admissions, and estoppels by the borrower to confirm the outstanding loan amounts and limit potential claims against the lender; releases, waivers, and covenants by the borrower not to sue the lender; and reaffirmation of the existing loan documents by all parties, including any guarantors and other secondary obligors.

The latter is very important, as the failure to obtain the consent of guarantors, indemnitors, or other secondary obligors might effectuate a partial or complete discharge of such parties. The documentation usually will include express modifications of the existing loan documents. Some of the modification documents may need to be recorded (such as modifications of the mortgage or deed of trust). The workout documentation will need to be signed, possibly acknowledged, and delivered. If the note is modified, an *allonge*—an addendum to the note—typically must be permanently affixed to the promissory note. Any amendment or modification to a mortgage or deed of trust must be recorded in the appropriate real property records, and any UCC financing statement must be filed in the proper UCC filing office. And, of course, the borrower will need to pay any fees or charges due to the lender and third parties for the modification before the workout closes.

Long Lead Items

Certain items need to be completed early to allow the closing to occur. Usually, a title policy endorsement is required (to ensure that the priority of the mortgage or deed of trust is not changed as against other creditors) if the mortgage or deed of trust is modified. The lender's counsel will have negotiated the form of any such endorsement and will arrange for its delivery (or the title company's commitment to deliver the endorsement) concomitantly with the delivery of the loan documents. Consents of third parties (such as mezzanine lenders or potentially even of a court, if the borrower has filed for bankruptcy protection) must be obtained before closing. Any cash management agreements and arrangements must be put into place (including notifying any tenants and obtaining the consent of any third-party bank to any control agreement providing the lender with control over borrower's bank accounts for the property).

Conclusion and Caveat

It is very important for a lender contemplating a workout to do its homework: It must bring in new counsel and, with counsel, analyze its business and legal position so that it understands what it would reasonably expect to collect in a foreclosure (and/or borrower bankruptcy) as compared to what it would reasonably expect to collect through a workout. To avoid increasing its potential liability, the lender must carefully document any actions it takes. Once its analysis is complete, if the lender moves forward to negotiate and document a workout agreement, it must make sure that all necessary loose ends are tied up: that all needed corrections to loan documents are made, that any needed consents are obtained in writing, that any filings are completed—because the workout provides the last best hope for a consensual resolution, and if it does not work, the lender will probably face litigation and much higher costs in order to collect on its loan.

One caveat: This chapter provides an overview of the mindset and key issues and tasks that must be handled by a lender in doing a workout. However, every lender has different internal and external priorities; and every project and borrower present their own challenges. For that reason, please note that this is a general guide, but not an exhaustive one. A short summary like this one cannot take the place of a full review of a specific loan and project done by competent businesspeople and experienced local counsel.

CHAPTER 7

Owners and Borrowers

Learn to Swim with the Sharks

As an owner of a commercial real estate property, you will experience many challenges in the years ahead. Even if you aren't one of the thousands that will be facing the daunting task of refinancing their commercial property, you will be confronting the changes of a marketplace reflecting the paradigm shift that has occurred. As you review the surveys provided by CoStar Group, you will see a consistent trend. With vacancy rates increasing and rental rates decreasing, combined with investor expectations rising in terms of expected returns that reflect the increased risk of the marketplace, values will inevitably be impacted in a negative manner.

If you are one of the owners confronting the possibility of a maturing commercial loan, an important rule is to start early and be vigilant in your research. If you obtained your loan in the peak years of 2004 through 2006, it's likely that your property no longer conforms to the underwriting standards used to originate your loan. Even if your property has the unlikely blessing of retaining its occupancy level and rental rates at the time of your loan's origination, increasing capitalization rates placing downward pressure on the value will still be a factor. Additionally, the restricted lending environment will likely continue to restrain the ability to refinance commercial real estate for some time to come, and interest rates are likely to increase due to competition for these loans.

If you're not prepared to refinance your property with the understanding that you will probably be required to invest additional capital into the property to meet the new market's loan-to-value standards, be prepared to sell it or begin the process of negotiating a loan modification or workout. You may be one of the thousands of owners who are experiencing increased vacancy or tenants requesting decreases in their lease rates, combined with the increasing capitalization rates.

If you own a property from which you operate your business, you are commonly referred to as an "owner/user." In that case, you may very well be experiencing reduced sales and trouble making your mortgage payments. Statistics show the average loan to value at time of origination for the loans that are coming due in the next three to five years is 70 percent. Considering the factors referenced above, the overall negative impact on values will likely exceed the original 30 percent investment. These combined factors will result in market conditions where the majority of commercial properties with maturing loans in the next several years will have existing debt exceeding their value.

We need cooperation and intervention from the commercial lending industry, regulatory agencies, and governmental representatives in order to create new standards for underwriting and amended regulatory guidelines.

These changes will be necessary in order to permit the kind of widespread, standardized loan workouts, extensions and modifications necessary to avert massive increases in defaults and foreclosures. The resulting increases in defaults and foreclosures would place even further downward pressure on values. While many larger investors, partnerships, REITs, and the like will have the capacity to make the additional investment necessary to obtain new loans, most typical owners of commercial real estate, owners of smaller properties, and owner/user buildings will not be in such a position. Therefore, they will be faced with the unfortunate options of either short selling (meaning a sale of the property at or below what is owed), negotiating some kind of loan modification with the existing lender, or allowing the properties to go back to the bank through foreclosure.

PRIDE OF OWNERSHIP AND PROPERTY MANAGEMENT RESPONSIBILITIES

So what's an owner to do? First of all, be vigilant in your property management and respect the responsibilities of ownership. Get professional assistance if necessary, but know that this paradigm shift in the marketplace is exemplified by the increased responsibilities and duties of an owner to properly maintain his or her properties and take better care to retain the any tenants. During the boom market such vigilance wasn't required of an owner. If a tenant failed to pay the rent, there was likely another tenant right behind it to replace it. Often, the new tenant would come into the building at an even higher rental rates. As an investor, if you had issues with vacancy, you could always sell the building and move your equity elsewhere.

Today, it's a different story. Tenants are asking for a reduction in rental rates en masse and these requests must be taken seriously. There are numerous ways to evaluate the individual tenant's concerns and make accommodations to facilitate its staying in the building. To ignore a tenant's request could very well be at the cost of the owner's own interests and the undoing of the property as a whole. This is not to say that as the owner you should automatically give a tenant everything it's asking for, but the demands and standards for property management are going to be much higher. When a tenant requests a decrease in its rent, a thorough review of the tenant's businesses, financial status, history of sales, and likelihood of survival will be necessary. Additionally, it may be prudent to take a number of other measures to assure that, if the tenant is viable and can stay, the restructuring of the lease has flexibility for future changes in the marketplace. A fair modification of the terms in the lease agreement will probably be less costly than the vacating of the space. The vacancy of the space creates the possibility of having to invest in additional tenant improvements, brokerage commissions, and the loss of income caused by the vacancy itself. Vacancies during the next several years will likely last longer than they have in the past.

I cannot overemphasize the need for owners to take a more active interest in the management of their commercial properties. If you have professional property, management oversight of the management company will also be critical to your success as a commercial real estate owner, since many of the market conditions will not have been seen before on such a massive scale. Keep in mind your property management company will be learning the new rules of this paradigm shift right along with you. Managing expenses, reviewing service contracts, making sure that competitive bids have been obtained for all services are critical to more effective property management. The marketplace will require various new tactics, and strategies that will be correlated to the geographic and demographic profile of each property and the related property type.

LOAN WORKOUTS AND LOAN MODIFICATIONS

If you find yourself owning a commercial building whose loan exceeds the value, or you are not sure what your position is, it will be important that you get professional qualified advice from a number of sources. To determine likely current value, consult with experienced commercial real estate brokers who have specific knowledge of your property and marketplace. Interview two to three different brokers and evaluate who has the credibility and experience necessary to assist you in the evaluation and analysis of your property. Proper preparation and valuation of your commercial property is a necessary and important component for consideration of a possible loan workout or loan modification. Next, you're going to want to seek the advice of legal counsel. Again, your legal counsel should be experienced in handling commercial loan workouts and negotiating loan modifications. Obtaining legal advice will assist in you in fully understanding the contractual obligations you made when you originated your loan. While most investors typically review their loan documents or have legal counsel review them when they take out a loan, few investors or borrowers were paying attention to the critical factors and details that will now play an important role with any effort to modify these commercial loans.

As the tsunami of loan maturities and resulting loan defaults rises, it is inevitable that companies will be formed to specialize in commercial loan modifications and loan workouts very similar to those that currently exist today for the residential sector. While owners must be wary and cautious of whom they choose to work with, as time goes by the leaders in this new industry will become evident and will likely serve an important role in resolving this crisis. I anticipate coordination with commercial real estate broker/consultants, legal counsel, and commercial mortgage bankers that work directly with the commercial loan servicers will be the most effective method of accomplishing a fair result for all involved. My web site www .tonywoodconsulting.com will track these services and refer clients to the most qualified experts in their area.

I would encourage every owner of commercial real estate to start early in its review and analysis of its property's value, debt exposure, and, in the case of tenant-occupied properties, the overall stability of the tenancy. Given the market conditions that we are currently experiencing and anticipate in the future, it's likely that a backlog and long delays (similar to what we have seen in the residential sector) will occur in terms of the lender's ability to review the requests for loan modifications and workouts. Unfortunately, unless you're in default on your loan, it's difficult to get a lender's attention to negotiate on existing loans. This is, in part, due to a combination of factors. A loan in default is categorized differently by lenders. Once it's in default, lenders have greater regulatory flexibility in negotiating on the defaulted loan. Unfortunately, throwing your loan into default simply to get your lender's attention and fairly negotiate with it on your troubled asset will have a detrimental effect on your credit rating. However, a foreclosure would be worse. Consulting with experts strategically is the key to successfully navigating this process effectively. Lenders also have a history of only addressing "fires" that must be put out and taking on the problem loans and troubled assets as they come to the Special Assets department. Hopefully, this kind of approach will change as lenders become more aware of market conditions that require them to become more proactive.

If the 2009 "test" of the largest banks included a more detailed analysis of the bank's commercial real estate loan portfolios, most would have failed.

So a bit of denial, and those three monkeys, "see no evil, hear no evil, speak no evil," are causing a drag on what could be a more efficient resolution of the problems at hand.

Hopefully, the commercial financing and commercial real estate industry's efforts toward achieving necessary changes, combined with governmental and regulatory participation, will result in establishing programs that facilitate the refinancing and loan modifications needed to avert further declines across the board in commercial real estate values.

NAVIGATING IN DANGEROUS WATERS: EXPERT GUIDANCE FROM COMMERCIAL LOAN WORKOUT SPECIALIST—MAURA O'CONNOR, SEYFARTH SHAW LLP

I knew whom I wanted as a contributor for the loan workout strategy portion of this book, but I had no idea what a contribution Maura O'Connor would make. Not only did Maura agree to an in-depth interview with me that spans everything from loan workouts to her thoughts on the overall U.S. economy (and our "bailout" mania), she also agreed to directly contribute sections of the book on loan workouts from both the lender's and borrower's points of view. For those of you who don't know Maura O'Connor, she is an intellectual powerhouse. If you spend any time with Maura or reading her blog on www.GlobeSt.com, you will always be in for an education and likely enjoy the process at the same time.

Maura is an attorney and partner in the Real Estate Practice Group in the Los Angeles office of the Seyfarth Shaw LLP law firm. Her practice focuses on real estate financing, acquisitions, development, and leasing. She has extensive experience in complex financing transactions, infrastructure and industrial projects, purchases of environmentally contaminated properties, and sophisticated real estate workouts and foreclosures. She has served as lead counsel for myriad senior and mezzanine loans, lease financings, securitized transactions, ground leases and equity investments for a wide variety of investors, banks, insurance companies, and others.

Ms. O'Connor has successfully handled the acquisition and entitlements of major retail, industrial, warehouse, and distribution facilities. She has designed large-scale systematized store site acquisition and leasing programs for retailers, most recently closing more than 150 store-site leases in 18 months for a new entrant into California and the United States. Maura is the Chair of the Los Angeles County Economic Development Corporation, and co-chairs its Strategic Land Use Committee. Ms. O'Connor frequently speaks on a variety of legal topics to business and legal groups. She was named one of the top 10 real estate lawyers in Southern California in 2005 by Real Estate Southern California, which also named her a "Woman of Influence" in 2006 and 2007. She has also been named as a Distinguished Alumna of the University of Minnesota Law School.

Ms. O'Connor is the author of the law blog, Practical Counsel, which offers her insights and commentary on legal matters related to commercial real estate. Practical Counsel is a joint publishing initiative with www .GlobeSt.com.

Tony Wood: Maura, let's start with CMBS financing and a borrower's ability to get a loan modification or a workout with the lender. I understand there are limitations to loan modifications, is that correct?

Maura O'Connor: Yes, but it depends on how troubled the loan is. A "Master Servicer" (which administers the loan prior to default or imminent default) has very limited rights to modify a CMBS loan. However, typically the pooling and servicing agreement provides broad rights to a "Special Servicer" (which takes over administration of the CMBS loan because the loan is in or very close to default) to modify the CMBS loan.

But once the loan has been transferred to the Special Servicer, it usually has the authority to modify the loan.

It may not be willing to do so in all cases: The Special Servicer ultimately has to answer to the investors. You need to draw a careful distinction between whether it has the ability to make a loan modification versus whether business reality permits it. Different tranches (classes) of investors in a CMBS pool have different interests.

For example, four different levels of investors might buy positions in a pool of CMBS debt. Each level has a different amount of risk—the investors with the least amount of risk will be entitled to less interest, and those with higher levels of risk will be entitled to more interest. That's an oversimplification, but here's the important point: The person who actually gets to direct the servicer is the lowest level risk holder (the one with the greater risk) that is "in the money" (based on the current information, will be likely to collect on its part of the payment stream from the loan).

TW: Define "gets to direct it"?

MOC: The person who is most likely to benefit or lose, based on where he or she is in the capital stack, will be the person or entity in the "first loss" position. That person or entity usually gets to instruct the servicer how to handle the workout, to the extent the pooling and servicing agreement does not do so. By the way, I'm using the term "workout" generically, to mean *anything* the lender does to change the original terms of the loan to come to a consensual deal to resolve the loan, including loan modifications, extensions, forbearance agreements, or complete loan restructurings.

TW: For the CMBS loans, I think that what's happening here—and likely to happen to the commercial real estate sector over the next few years—is almost a mirror image of what happened to the residential sector over the last several years. Do you see the similarity?

MOC: Yes. Frankly, the commercial real estate sector has been put into a bad position because of what happened in the residential sector. Many people borrowed and spent much more money than was prudent, using their home equity like an ATM. Businesses that were planning to buy or lease real estate made business projections for their *own* physical plant needs, based on their projections about what they could make and sell. Unfortunately, those projections were based on very inflated consumer purchase numbers. So the commercial entities over-bought (or over-leased) real estate for their own business needs.

Regulation may help defuse this. In September 2009, the IRS issued new interpretations of the rules applicable to REMICs (real estate mortgage investment conduits) to allow REMIC servicers to modify CMBS (commercial mortgage-backed securitized) loans over a longer period of time without triggering certain tax penalties. These changes, which were made retroactive to January 1, 2008, basically make workouts more attainable because they allow loan modifications by REMICs occasioned by "reasonably foreseeable" defaults.

TW: Let's step back a minute and talk about your firm as a whole and your business particularly. When did you notice the increase in demand for loan workout assistance? When did loan modifications and problems with loans spike up with people starting to come to you to request your assistance in negotiating something with lenders?

MOC: Our loan modification, workout, and foreclosure work picked up significantly last year, starting about January 2009. We had thought that there would be much more demand last year, but it did not materialize. In addition to federal governmental policies that have allowed lenders to "pretend and extend" rather than recognize their losses, it simply took a while for the bad state of the economy to work its way through to commercial real estate. For example, just because a retailer has a bad quarter doesn't mean that retailer can't pay rent; but if the retailer has enough bad quarters in a row, it may not pay rent or it may go out of business. Obviously, one retailer going under might not hurt a owner of a large shopping center badly enough to make it default on its debt—but if the defaulting retailer provided a large share of the shopping center's cash flow, its failure might trigger a loan default by the shopping center owner.

TW: Many borrowers have had difficulty getting lenders to listen to them unless their loans are actually in default. Many borrowers have been advised to miss a payment or two as a strategy to get their lender's attention.

Borrowers should be able to negotiate with their lender without throwing their property into default or foreclosures, right?

MOC: Borrowers shouldn't have to stop making their payments to get their lender's attention. Borrowers can usually get their lender's attention if borrowers make it very clear they are at serious risk of default fairly soon. What the borrower has to do is get somebody on the phone with the lender and, if necessary, be a complete nag (politely, of course) and say "Look, we're going to default if we can't work something out with you."

TW: What if borrowers can't make debt service payments?

MOC: Basically, there are two different types of situations: borrowers who can't make their monthly payments and those who have hit the maturity default and can't get refinanced. When they come to us, that distinction is important, because right now it's very hard to get new financing, partly because values have dropped and cap rates have increased, and of course, the CMBS market is either dead or on life support.

In all cases, it's helpful if the borrower has a realistic idea of what the property is worth. The lender will usually get an appraisal; the borrower is usually a lot closer to the property and has a better idea of what the property value (and potential) is. The borrower *should* know the cash flow and how much debt the property can actually support right now. A borrower usually needs a team, including a broker, legal counsel, and perhaps a finance expert. Some borrowers and developers have that kind of financial acumen themselves, but they can certainly hire experts if needed. You need somebody that can really run the numbers and understand the worth of the property based on cash flow, not based on comps, because right now nobody knows what the comps are.

TW: You know comps are like driving the car with the rearview mirror: They don't tell you what's going to happen, or what's happening today, they tell you what's happened in the last six months.

MOC: Comps are only one way of looking at a property's value. Cash flow is the more relevant method of valuation in a declining market, because it's really hard to tell what comps are relevant when few deals are closing.

TW: Do you have clients ask you, "Should we give the property back at this point or not?" if the value of the property has gone below what the borrower owes? I'm seeing people with tremendous net worth and good credit scores being willing to give properties back to the bank. Of course, they also want to protect their credit.

MOC: Yes. The big issue in most loans is: What does the lender or borrower have at stake? What can the lender expect to collect? If you have any obligation secured by real property in California, a lender can't just decide to go after the borrower because the property isn't worth anything. In California, unlike many other states, a lender almost always must foreclose first, pursuant to the "one action" and the "anti-deficiency" rules. There are two ways to foreclose on the real property: (1) non-judicial foreclosure, which takes about four months; and (2) judicial foreclosure, which can take longer. Each method has limitations. Usually, at the end of that four-month period in a non-judicial foreclosure, the lender gets the property but it can't go after the borrower for a deficiency (the difference between the value of the property and what was actually owed). For example, if you had a property encumbered by a $100 million loan and now the property is only worth $50 million, the "deficiency" would be the other missing $50 million.

However, if the lender has done its job with decent underwriting and has obtained competent guaranties and waivers, and if the loan is of a type where a judicial foreclosure is available, the lender often has the ability to do a judicial foreclosure. The trade-offs are that a judicial foreclosure will typically take one to two years, and after the lender gets the property back, it has a shot at getting that deficiency—but only after going through a fair value hearing (in which the court determines the intrinsic value of the property). And, in addition, the borrower has up to a year after the foreclosure sale to buy back the property by paying for it what the lender bid for it. So if there's an up-tick in the market, the borrower can buy it right back. In the meantime, the lender can't sell the property for a year and has to spend a lot of time and money on court proceedings. So most lenders prefer to do a non-judicial foreclosure in California.

Here is the real game, in the simplest possible terms: If the property is really under water and everybody agrees it's not worth anything, and the borrower has no equity, then it makes sense for the borrower to give the property back to the bank (either by deed in lieu or by agreeing not to oppose a foreclosure), limit its liability as much as possible, and pay as little money toward the guarantee as possible. That's scenario number one. An alternative scenario where the parties essentially agreed on the value of the real property collateral would be a consensual discounted payoff by the borrower. (Or a lender could just sell its note, and pass on the challenges of enforcing it to a buyer.)

In scenario number two, the lender thinks the property is under water, and the borrower disagrees. The borrower thinks there's real value in it, but doesn't want to put any more money of its own into it. The borrower just wants the lender to cut it a deal. That's when you see some big fights, and that's when you end up in litigation.

TW: When you say the borrower wants the lender to "cut it a deal," do you mean modify the loan?
MOC: Yes. If a property is far enough under water, typically the lender will not want to take it back. If it's only a little bit under water then the

lender will often *start* foreclosure proceedings, *but* will usually try to do a workout deal with the borrower where the lender gets paid off. Or they will try to work out a consensual resolution: maybe an extension, maybe a modification or a deal where the borrower puts in more money to reduce the lender's risk. The lender almost never wants to take the property back, and the lender wants to get paid. The lenders lend money, they want to get paid back money; they don't usually want to deal with real estate, and many lenders aren't very good at it.

A workout can be very simple or very complex. Some examples of simple loan workouts are the following: (1) The lender agrees to extend the loan for a few months and the borrower puts more money into the property; or (2) the lender agrees to extend loan for two years so that the borrower won't be in default until then (giving the borrower time in hopes that the economic climate will change for the better); or (3) the borrower will let the lender foreclose and will not hinder the foreclosure in any way. Another more complicated example: All parties agree the lender will foreclose (because there are legal reasons why a foreclosure is better than just taking back a deed to the property), and if the borrower agrees to cooperate, then lender will reduce borrower's principal's $20 million guarantee to $10 million, the borrower's principal agrees to pay the lender the $10 million, and the lender will forgive the borrower the other $10 million and won't damage the borrower's credit rating. In another more complicated workout, the borrower might agree to bring in new investors; the lender would get some part of its loan paid off and in exchange would give the borrower an extension.

Yet another possibility is to split the loan into two pieces. Then part of the loan keeps its priority and gets paid first, and part of the loan gets extended, and the borrower puts in new money, but the borrower's new money gets priority repayment ahead of the second part of the original loan.

Here's another more complex example: Some CMBS Special Servicers are starting to do modifications where the borrower brings in another borrower with more money who wants to take over the property, and the lender agrees to reduce the loan amount. For example, a $100 million loan might be reduced to $70 million, and the new borrower basically buys the property by assuming the $70 million loan. The lender takes the $30 million loss. The original borrower may even pay the lender a little bit more, say $5 million, for the lender's consent to the assignment to the new borrower, reducing the lender's $30 million loss by $5 million to $25 million.

There are really three big variables in these situations. One is *What is the value of the property?* That is determined based on the present value of the cash flow from the property, and what the property could sell for. Two: *Is there a guarantee and if so, what's its real value?* If the guarantor is bankrupt, the guarantee is probably worth nothing. If the guarantor has significant assets, its guaranty may be valuable. The third variable is *whether the people involved are reasonable*.

The reason it's difficult to standardize workouts is because there can be so many variables. When the value of the property is being disputed between the parties, and both sides have the money to fight—and the lender usually has the money to fight (the borrower may or may not)—you'll have litigation, and maybe even a borrower bankruptcy, and then everybody just bleeds money.

TW: However, isn't your firm anticipating a wave of foreclosures to deal with in the next few years?

MOC: Yes, we are. The commercial real estate players are probably not going to be able to move fast enough with modifications to fix all the problems. One of the things that we've done in our Los Angeles office is to create a systematized and scalable approach to commercial real estate foreclosures. One of my particular interests is streamlining the delivery of legal services so that our firm can deliver standardized legal services on a cost-effective basis. Seyfarth has developed a propriety business process approach: We have figured out how to deliver certain legal services that in a very standardized and scalable manner, frequently charging a fixed fee for a specific scope of legal work. This provides our clients with more predictable budget than the typical large law firm's approach of billing by the hour with no limitations. Most important, it allows us to tailor the services delivered to the needs of the specific client so that we can help it meet its business goals.

TW: When this wave of maturities hits, over the next three, four, or five years, well over a trillion dollars will become due and payable. As the inevitable foreclosures come about, the volume is likely to have a national impact. What about the "the guilt by association"—the impact on overall values seems likely to be significant, or am I missing something? The percent of gross national product (GNP) generated by the commercial real estate industry is 13 percent; that matters to the overall economic recovery, doesn't it?

MOC: This question is coming from a slightly different point of view for me, not wearing my real estate hat but my economics hat. I'm not an economist, but I watch a lot of economics data in connection with my volunteer work as Chair of the LA County Economic Development Corporation. So my opinions here reflect only my own opinion and not matters of law or opinions of any group I'm affiliated with.

The S&L crisis and resulting real estate crash in the 1990s took five or six years to get worked out. Some people got hammered and learned from it, some people were wiped out, and some people toughed it out and became better operators as a result.

Obviously, a big collapse in real estate values will hurt many people—owners of, financiers for, and service providers working in commercial real estate—but ultimately it may create some compensating benefits from an overall economic point of view for California and the United States as a whole. Real estate is a large cost factor for the average business. One of our challenges in California (as compared to the United States generally) is we're a high-cost place to do business, in part because real estate values have been bid up so high. If the cost of commercial real estate comes down, we may become a much more cost-effective place to do business. Businesses that actually create things to sell create the real wealth that drives the typical economy. As a nation, we have to buckle down, innovate, create, and start producing more things that the rest of the world wants to buy in more quantity. If real estate prices fall, we'd be more competitive as a manufacturing center that can produce goods, which we need to be.

As a country, we've been operating on the twin economic assumptions that consumerism actually drives the economy and doesn't hurt our economy. The latter was probably true when we were the world's largest creditor nation and built a lot of the goods we sold. Unfortunately, we've become the world's largest debtor nation. We are effectively in hock to China and the oil-producing companies, and as a debtor country, we have given our creditors a lot of power over our country. (We also have allowed our free trade policies to benefit producers in other countries who do not have to comply with environmental or labor laws like those of the United States. Economic theory says this is good policy in the long run, but I have reservations about it—as John Maynard Keynes said, we're all dead in the long run.)

We *could* probably lower our cost basis by changing our government's political policy of artificially propping up real estate prices, which makes it harder for people who might get into business because of their real estate costs. We *could* decide not to interfere with the workings of the economy, by letting the lenders that made really bad decisions go out of business, and by letting homeowners that made bad decisions to over leverage their houses to fund excessive spending go through foreclosure. (Of course, the government started pumping money into the financial industry to avert panic, and that risk might arise again.) Such corrective actions would hurt: Some lenders would go out of business; some former homeowners might have to rent for a while. Both lenders and homeowners may learn from this and even become more responsible in the future. That's a very tough thing to say, because obviously none of us wants to see people hurt—but there's not enough money in the world to re-inflate this bubble!

TW: Do you agree that we are going to have a lot more troubled commercial real estate and that values are going to be impacted across the nation?

MOC: Yes. I think we are going to see a significant increase in this area—unless Congress or the Administration changes how it's handling things. Nobody knows what the government is going to do next, because it seems to be designing a new bailout every few months.

The risk is that the government's intervention will extend the economic downturn or prolong the economic hit we have to take. Once we've stabilized the financial markets, as the administration says we have, the government should quit doing bailouts. The government may have made the right choice to do the bailouts to avert panic, but the question remains whether it can change strategies to a more economically rational strategy now that panic seems to have been averted.

Here's my concern: The effect of all these bailouts is the transference *to the taxpayers* of losses by lenders with imprudent lending policies and by homeowners with imprudent personal borrowing policies. Our political leaders have made the decision to hock our future tax receipts to provide bailouts to people and companies who took imprudent risks. I think this extraordinary strategy must—and should—end soon. However, *if* we are going to continue down the bailout path as a matter of public policy, then I think the government should also bail out the commercial real estate industry, which is a major driver of our economy.

TW: This is going to change the way people look at and evaluate risk for a very long time, I think.

MOC: I agree—and the question is *how* it should change the way they look at risk. Should each of us be incentivized to take all of the risks we want, however imprudent, knowing that the government—and ultimately our fellow taxpayers—will bail us out if we screw up—but we can keep our winnings if we have gains?

These bailouts are going to result in income and other taxes going up for the average person—and they will ultimately penalize those who did not benefit from imprudent risk taking. Ultimately, the social contract will break down if we go down that path. In addition, I think the stagnation caused by the lack of price discovery could have a deleterious effect on the whole economy—because people know that prices must come down and won't move forward with new business deals until they do. For those reasons, I personally don't think it's good policy to privatize gains and socialize losses.

TW: And of course it's too late—because we've already done it in a big, big way, haven't we?

MOC: The right question now is how much longer do we want to do it? Will we be allowed by our creditors to do it going forward? And should we, as responsible citizens, compound the problems, or should we instead make an effort to walk down a different path that leads to a more responsible future? We are where we are, and we can only make a choice about which path we should take going forward.

TW: As you look at the commercial real estate markets for 2010, what areas or property types are you most concerned about and what changes (regulatory or otherwise) will be helpful to the situation?

MOC: In its efforts to avoid panic, the government has overshot its goal by a bit: Its policies have encouraged lenders with problem loans to "pretend and extend," apparently indefinitely. As a result, although everyone in the industry knows that commercial real estate values have dropped significantly, there are not enough deals happening to have real price discovery.

Until there is real price discovery, stagnation will continue, and that may have very bad effects on unemployment and the larger economy. The higher unemployment gets, the worse for commercial real estate; obviously, unemployed folks don't need offices and buy less at retail.

Right now there are a lot of folks with cash waiting to do deals, but there is still a large gulf between the prices most lenders and other sellers are willing to sell at and the prices most buyers are willing to pay. The government's policy of shoveling virtually free money at financial institutions may have staved off panic in 2008. But I don't think it's the right strategy now.

My biggest concern is whether the government will timely change its strategy so that lenders are incentivized to start selling distressed loans and properties at market rates without panicking the markets. If the government moves too fast, panic may ensue. Alternatively, as CMBS loans mature, they may flood the market with properties and precipitate an overcorrection on the low end of pricing—which ultimately might hurt the very financial institutions that the governmental policy currently is designed to protect. However, if the government does not move quickly enough to change its strategy to promote realistic price discovery and the transfer of distressed assets at market prices, the ensuing stagnation may itself trigger another downturn in the larger economy. Such a downturn could continue the current economic malaise for years. That drag on economic growth could create even greater economic harm to many Americans (other than those in government-supported businesses) in the longer term than would a governmental strategy correction now. Fixing this mess definitely requires a deft balancing act by our government, and I am worried about whether our federal policymakers will be able to do so.

COMMERCIAL LOAN WORKOUTS FROM THE BORROWER'S PERSPECTIVE—MAURA O'CONNOR, SEYFARTH SHAW LLP

As default rates in commercial real estate loans have been increasing, we are seeing increasing defaults and resulting workout and foreclosure activity across our law firm's nationwide real estate practice. Some projects fail for reasons that are too difficult to resolve: For example, they may be too far under water to be saved. But many other distressed loans that result in foreclosures could have been worked out, if certain simple, and seemingly obvious, steps were taken by both sides, lender and borrower/developer, to cooperatively work out a consensual resolution. At the risk of stating the obvious, here's a brief overview of issues faced by borrowers in working out problem loans.

Borrower Mindset

Borrowers want to get their projects built and make a profit. And they usually come to a deal as optimists—they have to be, in order to get projects developed. Fundamentally, borrowers also are usually creative: They like designing projects and doing their work and are used to keeping control of their projects. One downside of this, in a downturn, is that some borrowers aren't quick to see themselves as in trouble, when a financed property starts to fall short of its covenants or cash flow. And even many of those who know that they are in trouble are hesitant to approach their lenders early, when trouble is foreseen but not yet happening, to seek a workout or forbearance. Instead, they may be tempted to act only after the trouble hits and their rents dry up, and then sometimes only by trying to obscure or shut down the flow of information to their lenders. This strategy generally does not work well.

Borrower Leverage

A borrower who knows its project is having cash flow or other problems should analyze its cash position, when it is likely to default on its loans, and what would be needed to get the project cash flowing again. This should be done as early as possible. It is usually advisable to bring in experts, such as asset managers, to help evaluate the financial position of the project, and lawyers, to help evaluate the borrower's legal position (strengths and weaknesses) and develop a strategy. This analysis will help determine if the borrower has any leverage it can use to negotiate a deal with its lender and what the lender's position is likely to be.

Finding Common Ground

As early as possible, but only after a careful analysis of the parties' positions and potential leverage, a borrower with a salvageable project should approach its lender and open discussions about working out the loan, confirming any oral requests in writing. If the lender is not responsive, the borrower should resend its request for workout discussions in writing, with a brief summary of its proposed workout plan, until it gets a response. (Using a lawyer can help—the borrower's lawyer can chase the lender's representative until a response is received.)

Most lenders won't enter into workout discussions with a borrower unless the borrower signs a "pre-negotiation agreement" or similar form. Usually, these agreements provide that, although the parties agree to talk about modifying the loan, there will be no change to the loan terms until they both agree to and sign formal loan modification documentation. Lenders require such letters to avoid any misunderstanding that they have agreed to some deal unofficially. Signing a short, reasonable pre-negotiation agreement should not be a problem for borrowers. On the other hand, some lenders try to materially improve their positions by including waivers of claims and defenses, full releases, and similar concessions in these agreements, so such agreements should always be carefully reviewed by a borrower's legal counsel before they are signed.

Once it gets the lender's attention, a borrower should consider proposing a plan likely to work over a reasonable time that, if possible, does not require the lender to put more money into the project. In exchange for a loan modification and more time to pay off the loan, borrowers might consider offering any or all of the following concessions, or any others specifically tailored to the project:

- Borrower or its principals may put in more equity.
- Borrower or its principals may sell shares in the project to investors, giving up some upside.
- Borrower may agree to defer any payments to itself or any affiliates.
- Borrower may provide the lender with other collateral.
- Borrower may scale back the quality and expense of the tenant improvements it wants to put into the project.
- Borrower may agree to sell other properties to raise cash to put into the troubled project.
- Borrower may propose giving back the property to the lender in exchange for a release or limitation of liability of borrower and/or its guarantor.

The point of offering such concessions is to limit the lender's loss exposure and thereby incentivize the lender to extend and modify the loan. While such concessions may be painful to consider, a rational borrower will almost always be better off starting with its own list of suggested scaling down changes, rather than a less informed or more painful list that its lender might confect.

A lender may or may not provide detailed comments on a borrower's workout proposal—generally, lenders are not willing to tell the borrowers what to do, as they are usually concerned about not incurring lender liability for taking over a project. But a rational lender ought to be able to let its borrower know what about the borrower's proposal works for the lender and what doesn't. Then, if the parties find common ground, they and their lawyers can negotiate a modification and extension that puts the loan and the project back on track.

What Not to Do

Here's a summary of obvious missteps to avoid in an early stage workout.

1. Lie to the other side, threaten your lender, or act so unreliable that they can't put trust in you. (This includes making inaccurate statements or unfulfilled promises through your lawyer.)
2. Become silent and unresponsive.
3. Ask for something before analyzing your real economic position (you may be asking for the wrong thing).
4. Start the conversation too late to have any viable options for returning the deal to a performing, healthy one.
5. Ask the other side to do your work for you.
6. Be rude (or allow your lawyer to be rude) to the other side's people and other representatives.

Knowing the Property

Borrower/owners usually are in a far superior position to a lender in understanding what it takes to run, and profit from, the real estate and its related operating assets. Normally, the lender looks to the owner, or his operator managers, to know how best to keep the property performing and adequately maintained.

The bottom line here is that, in an early stage workout, property owners should try to continue to be the "experts" for themselves and lenders both, and anticipate problems. In that role, owners can offer solutions or compromises on any problem areas, and keep the momentum going in the project, forestalling the lender from considering trying to take over and bring in someone else (like a receiver).

Cash Flow Considerations

In a workout, cash is king. A smart lender will look at these issues right away, so as a borrower, you want to be ahead of the game here as well.

Obviously, a failure to keep up with required debt service on the loan will trigger payment defaults and is the common path to a tough workout. But other cash issues must be kept in mind as well.

It's entirely reasonable in an early stage workout to try to reduce operating expenditures to the necessary minimums. Troubled borrowers sometimes are counseled to slow pay or shut down some nonessential items to build a cash kitty, which might be used to reduce the secured debt and forestall enforcement or foreclosure.

However, failure to pay necessary maintenance, utilities, insurance, or similar costs could trigger waste or covenant defaults, or even "bad boy" recourse or guaranty provisions. (Shut down utilities, for example, and you may lose fire/life safety protection, or suffer mold due to HVAC being down.) Shorting unsecured trade creditors also might alienate them, reducing the chance that this class of creditors would be friendly to the borrower in a later bankruptcy and support a reorganization plan that would keep current ownership in place.

Distributions of cash to an owner or partner, even prior to default, can be problematic in a workout. This is because bankruptcy law (and some other remedies) may give a lender, and other creditors, some rights to claw back those funds later. Any plans of a borrower/owner to make payments to owners or insiders should be carefully discussed with legal counsel if a workout or default is approaching.

Intrinsic Value of the Property

Again, this is something a sophisticated borrower may understand much better than the lender (even though the lender will almost certainly order an appraisal). Remember, the lender is not necessarily expert in what makes your specific property special. The borrower needs to highlight for the lender the unique features of the property, as well as the reasons why the borrower is the best person to run the property in a way that makes the best out of those unique features in the long run, even if there's difficulty in the short run.

At a risk of stating the obvious, a borrower should figure out its position and points of leverage before proposing a workout to its lender. (Frequently, borrowers give up points of leverage without getting anything in return because they don't want to spend the time or money analyzing their business and legal positions.)

Review the Loan Documents (Including Guaranties and Correspondence) or Have New Counsel Do So

It's a good idea to bring in new counsel to look at the deal documents, because new counsel will bring in fresh eyes and will be able to see what's *actually written* in the loan documents, *rather than* what counsel that did the original deal *thinks was done*. (It's simply human instinct to see what one thinks is there.) Obviously, the new counsel should be experienced in real estate workouts in the state where the property is located, as there are many subtle state-specific legal issues that affect the borrower's and lender's respective rights when a real estate loan is being enforced.

It is not uncommon for loan documents to contain flaws that could affect their enforceability—or could at least give the borrower some leverage in a workout. About one out of every two or three deals we see dating from loans made from 2005–2007 has had at least one major documentation problem that could be used by a borrower to increase its leverage. For example, a few problems I've seen over and over in twenty years of practice are the failure to attach the proper legal description; inadequate or ineffective guaranty waivers; ineffective or incomplete transfers of notes (from one lender to another); and incorrect UCC filings. (The latter can be very important in loans secured by certain asset types: You can't run a hotel after foreclosure without its beds, furniture, etc.). Also, sometimes correspondence with the lender will disclose that the lender agreed to do certain things, and has not done so; this can also provide leverage to the borrower.

Basically, a business and legal review of the property and the loan documents should be done to fix any potential defaults or similar problems the borrower can fix (such as a failure to deliver required information that could trigger a default) and to develop leverage. That allows the borrower to make a proposal reflecting a practical solution to the problems facing the property that is likely to be accepted by the lender.

Maintenance and Waste

Early in a workout, a key issue for borrower/owners will be to make sure that the property is not being "wasted" (generally having its value significantly diminished by lack of care).

Specifically, borrowers should assess and confirm that the condition of the property doesn't deteriorate to where it triggers covenant breaches that make it more likely the lender will foreclose rather than doing a workout.

Also, it's fairly common for "non-recourse" loans to have a "bad boy" carve-out recourse provision or guaranty, reimposing personal liability on the borrower or on a guarantor for some grave defaults, such as significant waste. In such cases, it's in the borrower's (or guarantor's) interest not to risk personal liability by letting the improvements start to fall apart.

Insurance Coverages

Financed owners should check their casualty and liability insurance coverage for the property, to confirm that adequate coverage is in place; premiums are paid; and all needed policies are up to date, in force, and sufficient to satisfy any loan covenants about mandatory minimum coverage.

Other Areas of Personal or Pass-Through Liability

Another set of issues, where the borrower should analyze the situation and try to get ahead of the game, is any other loan document clauses that give the lender direct right against assets beyond the property itself—like the borrower's principal (if the borrower is a corporation, LLC, or other entity) or any guarantors.

At the outset of a possible workout, a borrower should carefully check whether:

- There is an unfulfilled capital contribution obligation, a possibility of future mandatory capital calls.
- There is an argument that the property's ownership vehicle is under-capitalized and can be ignored (sometimes called "veil-piercing"), and liabilities passed through to the next level of ownership.
- There is personal liability for real estate taxes.
- There is a guaranty (or arrangement that amounts to a guaranty) that can be called.
- The legal fees incurred by one party in a default or workout must be reimbursed by, or can be demanded from, the other side.
- If an investor and developer are in partnership (or similar arrangement), what further calls or liability can be placed on the investor.
- Whether officers, directors, or partners have personal liability for actions taken or not taken—and whether directors' and officers' insurance is in place to address those risks.
- What exactly has been granted as collateral for the loan? There may be omissions that the lender will wish to see corrected. A borrower can sometimes agree to correct such omissions in exchange for concessions it needs to work out the loan and return the project to profitability.

Consider All Options

The property securing the loan may be so far under water that the best possible option is to work out a deal with the lender to give the property back to the lender (either through a deed in lieu of foreclosure, or through an agreement not to oppose the lender's foreclosure), possibly in exchange for a limitation or cancellation of any personal liability of the borrower and/or any guarantor. It may make sense to make a sacrifice sale of one project to keep others, or the borrower's company, afloat. The sooner a borrower can stop bleeding cash flow, the more likely it is that it will survive the recession. While it is difficult emotionally to consider such grim options, borrowers that are willing to make a cold appraisal of the value and marketability of their projects and all options for handling them are typically much better able to negotiate more favorable outcomes in workouts with lenders by moving quickly and rationally toward an outcome that works adequately, if not well, for both parties.

There's No Substitute for a Thorough Review and Analysis of the Loan Documents

Only a thorough legal review up front by experienced local real estate workout counsel will give the borrower the understanding of its situation and potential liability. Such an understanding will allow the borrower's principals to do a thorough business review and then to understand what the best possible outcome is—and to negotiate a workout or other resolution that moves as much in that direction as possible under the circumstances.

CHAPTER 8

Buyers
Beware of Hidden Debris

The Cycle of Market Emotions (see Figure I.1 in the Introduction) was created by Westcore funds and fundamentally lays out the roller coaster ride of investors. From Optimism to Capitulation and back to Optimism, timing is everything. However, waiting too long for a "good deal" can have you miss the opportunities in the market today for the possibility of a better deal in the future. Greed can be your friend or your undoing. Be clear about what you wish to accomplish; if you are looking for a building you wish to occupy for your business, there are certain parameters you must satisfy in combination with your search for an undervalued asset. If you are looking strictly as an investor, you are limited by your capital investment criteria and property type familiarity.

BUYERS IN THE TSUNAMI MARKETPLACE

As a prospective buyer in this newly established marketplace, the term "buyer beware" has never been more relevant. Whether you are purchasing a million-dollar office building or a $30 million mixed use development, if you are buying the asset or the note from a lender's Special Asset or REO department, or directly from the principal of the distressed asset, you cannot be too careful in your diligence to determine the challenges and unforeseen problems the property in question may possess. When entering the market now, under these conditions, you would be well advised to tread cautiously. It will be important to obtain sufficient knowledge and expertise through appropriate sources and representations so as to avoid the pitfalls, risks, and hazards that will be easily hidden from even the most experienced commercial real estate investors.

Many who have seen some success in the residential sector may try their hand in the new commercial market. Prospective purchasers who have not delved into the world of commercial real estate must be sure to do their homework first. Commercial real estate is like a different planet compared to residential, and appreciating the nuances and different approaches used in commercial real estate investment is necessary to make an accurate assessment of your investment opportunities. For those more experienced commercial real estate developers and investors, beware of the blindness your previous experience may cause. That was then; this is now. The rules for success established during the boom cycle will not translate well in the years ahead. Your previous success may interfere with your judgment. Driving a car while looking into the rearview mirror doesn't work here either. Remember, this is a paradigm shift marketplace, and the rules have changed, so some amount of reeducation is necessary even for the most experienced investors.

Whether you are buying a defaulting note from a lender, properties in default, or those already taken back by the lender through foreclosure, obtaining critical, complete, and accurate information on the existing condition of these assets as a buyer is difficult. The lenders involved will only have access to a limited amount of information on their distressed assets. Factual data about deferred maintenance, the physical and fiscal conditions of a given property, and the like may have been lost when the previous/original owner/borrower surrendered the property to the bank. Lenders do not follow the same standard as buyers to obtain due diligence information on their portfolios of properties in default or those taken back in foreclosure. When a property goes into default or otherwise gets the attention of a lender's Special Asset or REO department, it tries to obtain what it can from a borrower about the subject property. Unfortunately, for reasons ranging from self-protection to bad record keeping, the borrowers typically only provide limited, incomplete records and documentation on the physical and financial condition of the property. Each lender has its own policy and procedure with regard to managing these special assets, and they change from lender to lender; in some cases on a daily or weekly basis. Some lenders' Special Asset departments are overwhelmed, and they will likely become even more so as the huge wave of commercial real estate loan maturities hits increasing default rates over the next few years. Many lenders may not have sufficient personnel on staff in their Special Asset departments to manage the increasing wave of defaulting loans and related properties. It seems inevitable; lenders will restructure their Special Asset departments to function more efficiently in the management and disposition of their special assets. Currently, lenders who have special assets that are particularly problematic will seek out or otherwise entertain offers to purchase these notes at significant discounts. Typically, these are all cash transactions with very short due diligence. Not for the faint of heart.

BE A SMART BUYER—DO YOUR HOMEWORK FIRST

I have observed buyers, not fully advised of the marketplace, purchasing property at 2007 values in 2009, 50 percent over what the market value was. Why? Because they did not do their homework, and they did not have appropriate representation. Unfortunately, they may be some of the first to need assistance and will hopefully have better success obtaining the information they need to mitigate their damages. Finding competent, experienced, knowledgeable professionals in commercial real estate brokerage is critical to your success in the purchase of property offered on the open market or negotiating directly with the bank or lender on an REO. You can obtain this assistance via consulting agreement, paying a flat fee or on an hourly basis or with a representation agreement that incorporates a brokerage fee to be paid at the close of escrow.

CASH IS KING

"Cash is king" has quickly become a common saying anywhere you go, from buying a car to buying a house to buying an office building or shopping center. If you have the liquid assets necessary to pay all cash for the commercial real estate you are seeking to purchase, you will be in a particularly strong position. Anyone selling real estate today is not interested in waiting for 60 to 90 days to determine if the lender of your choice will be able to deliver the loan promised and necessary to close a transaction. Therefore, exceptional discounts are available to those who have the cash and can close quickly. Lenders in the sale of their foreclosed properties are particularly interested in entertaining offers from buyers with cash to complete their purchases. So be prepared and use your ability to pay all cash to your advantage.

"I want to buy a commercial foreclosure property on the courthouse steps."

Those of us in the commercial real estate brokerage industry have heard this many times from prospective buyers. These buyers have been told by friends, family, or a guy in a seminar to go directly to the courthouse steps to participate in the auction sale of repossessed real estate and reap the benefits that you otherwise cannot obtain in the general marketplace. This could not be further from the truth.

In fact, not only is this inaccurate advice, but it will also thwart a prospective buyer from having full access to the many opportunities available in the marketplace. Many opportunities in the open marketplace will be superior to what you would find on the courthouse steps. Besides, most buyers are looking for a particular kind of property with specific criteria. Most buyers are interested in owning in a particular area or demographic. By limiting yourself to what you can find at a courthouse auction, you are limited to whatever happens to be for sale at the time at that particular auction. I'm not saying that you can't find opportunities on the courthouse steps. I'm just saying it isn't the most efficient way to find a good investment opportunity in commercial real estate. It is not an effective or useful way to spend your time or money. Additionally, it's important to realize that there are groups of professional investors that specialize in nothing else but these courthouse types of purchases. It's very complicated, there are numerous risks, and you'd better have a series of cashier's checks to participate in the bidding.

I remember in the 1970s, the term "the 40 thieves" was used to apply to those who would regularly attend these foreclosure auctions, and how sometimes they would conspire to outbid a particular novice investor attempting his first shot at buying on the courthouse steps. If you do decide you want to give it a shot, be sure to get well-educated about the process and obtain proper representation prior to showing up to these auctions.

Depending on the marketplace, you will likely find better opportunities in the open market than the limited number of properties that actually end up on the courthouse steps.

I can assure you in the coming months and years there will be many properties for sale in the open market. Troubled assets, commercial short sales, owners in default needing to sell vacant properties, and REOs (real estate owned) taken back by banks will be on the market and ready to entertain your offers with a much more straightforward process. This process is easier to understand and easier to navigate which is an important consideration before you limit yourself to what you can find on the courthouse steps.

HAIR ON THE DEAL—THE IMPORTANCE OF DUE DILIGENCE

Due diligence is always an important consideration in any real estate transaction. The commercial real estate property has a variety of variables that must be looked at and considered during the due diligence. Each property type will have some of the same and some very different areas to investigate. Obtaining proper financial data, tenant profiles, leases, service contracts, and copies of all pertinent documentation related to the property including structural and environmental reports and physical inspections are standard operating procedure in any commercial real estate transaction. The challenge of completing a thorough and accurate investigation during the due diligence process for property that has been in default for a long time before it was taken back by the lender can be an onerous task.

Many times properties that are sold under market value will be said to have "hair" on them. This term is one of many used to describe a situation where property has an additional burden that must be addressed outside of the norm. Sometimes it's a building whose construction has not been completed. It may be a retail center that lost its anchor. Deed restrictions, code violations, construction defects, ingress and egress or easement issues, owners' associations—the list goes on and on. It's not unusual to find a property for sale that has some kind of hair on it, some kind of challenge, that may need to be addressed. These concerns take on a whole new level when you go to purchase a property that is in default, offered as a short sale, or has been otherwise repossessed by a lender.

It simply goes with the territory of distressed assets that there are issues with the property. Some will be evident, such as the entire building is vacant or the construction has not been completed and there is no certificate of occupancy. It's the issues that will not be visible or otherwise evident and unknown to a lender who has taken the property back that can really hurt you as a prospective owner. Val Berlin Douglas, aka Val The Title Gal with North American Title, reminds us, "Many times, the unseen issues are related to title. So it's critical that you have adequate title policy coverage, possibly purchasing additional endorsements that can protect you from the unknown." There are many title issues that do not present problems for a lender but can hurt an owner or buyer of a property. For example, Maura O'Connor was reviewing title for a retail acquisition and found that the sole access for the shopping center was through an easement over a culvert, and that easement would expire in 15 years. The lender, which was making a 10-year loan, did not care. But a buyer would have to arrange for an extension of the easement or another solution. If there are tenants in the building, tenant interviews and estoppels confirming the leases and their terms would be highly recommended. If there is an owners association, obtain a minimum of three years' books and records and make sure you read the minutes from the meetings. You may be surprised by a perfectly good-looking building and how it can be negatively impacted by the activities of an owners association in disarray or under the threat of a lawsuit.

Remember properties typically have fallen into default or have gone back to the bank for a reason (or several reasons), and it's critical you find out what that reason was and if you can overcome it. Overleverage can be solved by buying low, but a bad location cannot be fixed. Before your due diligence expires and you proceed to close of escrow, make sure you're comfortable with your understanding of all the problems (risk) associated with owning this property and your ability/willingness to take on the burden of solving them. In purchasing distressed or REO property, the fundamental discount must correlate to the resolution of the issues the property presents. Complete your due diligence properly and thoroughly and negotiate to obtain the necessary discount in price to mitigate your risk. If you follow these rules, you will be better equipped to achieve your commercial property investment goals, and your probability of success will have been increased tremendously.

CHAPTER 9

Commercial Real Estate Brokers

Charting a New Course in a
Paradigm Shift Marketplace

As a commercial real estate broker for more than 30 years, I have seen my share of "bad market" cycles. As a result, I have developed a reputation for looking outside the box of typical brokerage methodologies when necessary and applying a good share of creativity to get the job done. Many brokers in the commercial real estate marketplace today are struggling with what is happening and how to move forward. Sales and leasing activity in most metro markets have fallen off a cliff, and we haven't hit bottom yet. Many brokers are feeling lost and even the most successful are saying, "I haven't seen anything like this before, have you?"

I would not presume to have the answers for every broker in each market across this country, yet I knew it was critical that this book offer substantive ideas for addressing the kinds of concerns commercial real estate brokers are facing. How do you sell when there are no sales occurring? Who do you represent when there is no one in the market? As the market conditions got progressively worse during 2009, my work got noticeably more time consuming and difficult. More and more the bulk of my activity was problem solving for lenders, owners, and tenants alike. While my phone kept ringing, what I was hearing was clients with a lot of questions about what was going on. Then more questions. They needed my assistance dealing with losing tenants, the limited activity, and the loss of value to their properties. Then the tenants would call for assistance in renegotiating their leases or moving out of their space and "downsizing." I wanted to be of service, but I also needed to earn a living. I was spending hours, days of my week with clients who didn't want to buy, sell, or lease in this market; they just needed answers. While I continued to be successful in my work representing lenders on the sale of their commercial REOs, the overall volume in the market was falling like a rock. I wondered, "How are agents going to make it in this market?" and "How are the commercial brokerage firms going to survive?" I knew if things didn't change, it could be years before we would see the level of market activity rise enough to generate the brokerage fees necessary for commercial brokerage firms to stay afloat.

Given these unusual market conditions, the answers don't lie in anti-quated sales techniques like "smile and dial" and "fake it till you make it." We must take our knowledge and expertise and apply new strategies purposefully designed to effectively navigate these unknown territories and find our way to the other side. It is going to take more than hard work and determination. Hard work and determination are fine, but they must have a practical and effective application or you will just end up tired and frustrated (and broke).

We are in a paradigm shift marketplace where the rules are not clear and some have yet to be written. For help I turned to someone who may not have all the answers but could help me see what questions we should be asking. He is someone who knows a lot about being a commercial real estate broker and running a commercial real estate brokerage firm: His name is Tom Loeswick. Tom's business coaching approach is one of the few systems that are applicable in today's unique marketplace. His guidance in finding an accurate perspective and developing strategies for success can help those who are lost find their way to a better place in their marketplace. What I particularly like about Tom's approach is that it's not just about today and tomorrow—it's about planning to succeed into the future. His quiet demeanor is grounded with a calm confidence of his knowledge and a clear love of the work he does to support others in their business endeavors. It has been a pleasure getting to know him and watching him work.

Tom Loeswick is a Partner and Business Coach with Shirlaws, a global business coaching firm. He has extensive experience in coaching brokers, brokerage firms, and real estate advisors. He has 25 years of experience in the commercial real estate industry, including being owner of Sterling Advisors, a real estate advisory firm, Chairman of Colliers Parrish, in the Silicon Valley (one of the most competitive markets in the world), and he has been involved in advising and representing institutional investors of real estate in over $2 billion in transactions. He attained "Broker of the Year" status in the Silicon Valley and has a reputation as the consummate professional in whatever he does.

The following section, Perspective and Strategy for Brokerage Firms and Brokers, Tom Loeswick generously submitted with contributions by his associates at Shirlaws, Darren Shirlaw and Marc Johnstone and support from Rebecca Young.

PERSPECTIVE AND STRATEGY FOR BROKERAGE FIRMS AND BROKERS: A COACH'S VIEW— TOM LOESWICK, SHIRLAWS

When we ask commercial real estate brokerage companies about the impact of this recession on their revenue—the answer we consistently hear is that *business is off by 70 percent.* The recessionary economy, and the subsequent impact on the commercial real estate market, is still in the early stages of impact. Vacancy rates are expected to continue to rise, and sales will be sluggish until the market bottoms out.

So how do brokers and brokerage companies successfully navigate this challenging environment?

To get perspective on this environment we must first look at how these cycles typically work. In all of the recessions since the Great Depression there have been four fundamental phases:

- The Down—the severe correction of the market and significant losses.
- The Drag—the period where the market moves up and down in a minimal range but never achieves a sustainable recovery.
- The Release—this a retest of the previous downward cycle.
- The Up—this is the long upward trend.

So it looks like Figure 9.1.

The 70 percent drop in revenue does not reflect the reality of the market. Some markets have gone dormant and others are still operating, albeit at a substantially reduced volume. Specifically:

- Sales brokers will experience the biggest impact—investment sales have all but stopped.
- For tenant rep brokers and agents who list space—fewer tenants, lower rents combined with substantially shorter terms means substantially lower revenues.
- Listing brokers continue to have severely reduced income as a large volume of vacant space will not be absorbed anytime soon.

So what is it that brokers can do doing this Drag Period?

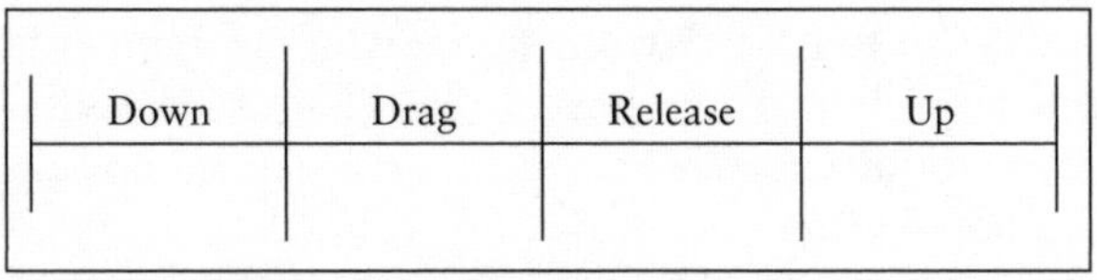

Down	Drag	Release	Up

FIGURE 9.1 Fundamental Phases of a Recession
Source: Shirlaws™

Become Efficient

Brokers and brokerage companies must get their efficiencies worked out. The overhead cost must be driven below cash flow or breakeven in order to have some money to invest in developing new strategies, service lines, and marketing approaches. Many firms and brokers cut back, but never far enough, leaving them unable to maneuver in a critical time in the market.

Repackage

Once efficiencies are squared away, the broker and the brokerage company must look to repackage service lines to match what owners and tenants are looking for in this special market. After the down and into the Drag Period, most brokers find they are trying to sell *boom services* in a *recessionary market*. Boom services are those services that sold very well before the recession. *Recessionary products match the desire to cut costs, restructure, and navigate uncertainty.* Winners in this climate will focus on:

- Cost saving services such as tax appeal, tax segregation, and expense management service.
- Lease restructuring that blends and extends the current lease rate— trading term for a lower rate and landlord security.
- Lease termination or surrender.
- Debt restructure or surrender.
- Equity restructure or surrender.

Turn Repackaging into Income through Positioning and Volume Plays

Once the service lines are repackaged there is still work to do turn the repackaging into income. The reality is there are substantially fewer transactions being done—especially at the beginning of a property market recession. There are two keys to successfully navigating through this tougher part of the cycle:

- *Positioning*—A repackaged product must be positioned in a way that allows the broker to hold a strong position in the mind of your prospective clients. How many times have brokers heard the feedback "they are all so good" or "about the same as other brokers," and the selection is then solely based on price.
- *Volume* is key to a successful outcome by designing how to make money in the Drag Phase of the market. Many brokers are still employing a

one-to-one cold calling or referral approach to attract new business. *The sales ratios change during the Down and the Drag Phases.* Prospects and clients are less decisive, timing is an issue, and waiting is many times easier than making a decision in a deteriorating market. Therefore, prospecting activities must be designed to create a broader audience and generate a higher number of prospects in order to have enough clients that are ready to transact.

At Shirlaws we look at Revenue Generation using the Model in Figure 9.2.

During this dramatic change in the market it is important for firms to review their entire business model to make sure each area is contributing rather than inhibiting the sales process. With real estate companies we discuss:

- *Products*—Your service lines of leasing, sales, appraisal, property management, and other offerings of commercial real estate brokers.
- *Positioning*—Who you are relative to the competition. Is your core skill creating and delivery product/services or is it building relationships? Are you focused on market, service, product, or price to differentiate yourself?
- *Distribution*—Your channels to market; this is your source of new prospects. How many sources do you have and what is the quality of the prospects or leads that you get? We measure the quality in two ways:
  - Are they pre-sold? Are the prospects you see ready to hire you or are they cold leads with whom you need to establish credibility and compete for their attention?

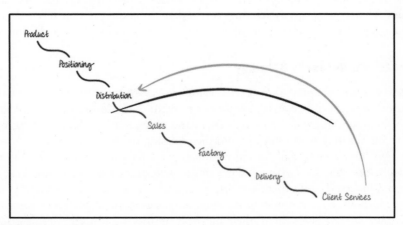

FIGURE 9.2   Shirlaws' Revenue Generation Model
Source: Shirlaws™

- Are the leads pre-qualified? Do these leads match the type of prospects you are looking for, your specialty, or ideal client profile? Do you keep attracting prospects that are outside of your expertise or interest?
  - *Sales*—Are you converting the prospects that match your offering? We have found that many brokers spend time selling, coercing, or working with clients that are unlikely to buy their offer. The sales process is really about creating and deepening the relationship.
  - *Product Design/Strategy*—Product design is about customizing your service to the clients' situations or requirements.
  - *Product Delivery*—For actually marketing a space, selling a building, or representing a tenant, do you have a consistent process that brings the best people to the table at each stage of the transaction?

Are there multiple touches in the process where the client experiences significant value? Is loyalty built with each touch?

  - *Client Service*—What are you doing to energize the relationship outside of the transaction? Do you have a strategy for how you energize clients as well as a priority for whom you focus on? Have you defined specific "extras" that deepen your relationship?

Most managers we talk to tell us they have a sales issue. We find the source of their issues actually occurs long before the sale. If they don't have the right products packaged to match the market's appetite, presented and delivered in a way that positions them positively against the rest of the competition, and if they don't have lead sources that generate pre-sold and pre-qualified leads—the result is low sales volume.

Energizing sales entails getting to the source issue(s) that are the block to sales. That is why simply focusing on markets, cold calling, and selling techniques alone rarely work or build a sustainable and highly successful business.

Creating a Recovery Strategy

Most firms will wait too long to develop a clear strategy for how they will profit from the recovery. It's analogous to waiting too long to get out of the stock market and losing a lot to a crash and then compounding the error by waiting too long to get back in and then missing the recovery!

We have found that *the source issue here is people's personal and business risk profile.* Every person has a risk profile. Some are more comfortable with taking risk and others are not.

Shirlaws has our clients measure themselves through a risk profile assessment that gives them, their business partners, and executives a clear sense of each person's risk profile.

We measure risk on a 0–10 scale as shown in Figure 9.3.

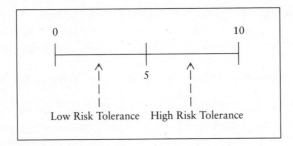

FIGURE 9.3 Risk Tolerance

Source: Shirlaws™

- 0 represents those who are unwilling to take any risk with their capital. These are the people that are more comfortable putting their money under a mattress.
- 10 represents those who are totally focused on big returns and the risk of losing their investment capital is not a major issue. These folks would be comfortable investing in oil wells in Iraq.

Those with lower risk profiles will be slower to invest in recovery strategies. Those with higher risk profiles are usually more willing to invest early. The market has shown over and over that those that are ready to implement new strategies at the beginning of the recovery do it at a lower cost and get a substantially higher return, Designing and building a robust strategy can take 9 to 12 months of planning and training.

We recommend that our clients put together their Recovery Strategy during the Drag Period (once efficiencies and their recessionary revenue model are squared away). *If a business hasn't agreed on a risk profile that it will use to make major business decisions, then boards, managers, and brokers can find themselves deadlocked.* Those who are comfortable with more risk, say a 6 to 8 on the Shirlaws scale, will likely be willing to invest in building strategy early during the Drag Period. Those that are risk averse, below 5 on the scale, will likely be late to the party and are much more likely to lose market share in the recovery.

Where are the biggest opportunities that will show up as the market recovers?

The current recession and shifts will cause some major restructuring of markets. Certainly, the most noteworthy is the collapse of the credit market colliding with a significant increase in vacancy and falling rental rates. Perhaps the biggest impact to brokers will be one of the brokers' biggest assets—his or her long-term relationships. *There will be a complete changing of the guard around those relationships that control debt and equity.*

This will impact:

- The investor market—New advisors will become active;, some old ones will fail.
- The equity market—New relationships will be made with equity partners.
- The debt market—A whole new game: How much debt will be available is anybody's guess.
- Loan brokers—Many long-term relationships will disappear and new ones will be made.
- Investment property brokers—There will be an initial wave of very short term investors followed by a second wave of midterm hold investors. Making the right relationships early will likely set the stage for the next three to five years of business.
- Tenants—Will get new landlords.

The ways that capital, in the form of debt and equity, get to the market and who is providing it will change dramatically.

Some long-standing investors and lenders will go out of business, go through massive restructures or takeovers as a result of the substantial repricing of assets.

At the beginning of a cycle like this, many of the current people and roles seem to hold up. However, when the major repricing hits, and the time frame for the recovery draws out the business failures, early retirements and layoffs usually increase at a dramatic pace.

An example: In 1991, the real estate market in Silicon Valley started into a deep recession. There were nearly 900 brokers working the market at that time. The phrase in that market correction was "stay alive until 95." However, most brokers didn't have the market traction or financial capability to hold on that long. By the middle of 1994 the number of brokers had dropped to approximately 300. Two-thirds of the brokers had left the market! This is likely to be the case again, as this correction is expected to be as deep and last at least as long.

Some managers of real estate firms believe their major role is to simply survive this downturn. In actuality that is only half of the story. The key opportunity is to use this downturn and recovery to reposition the firm. If you are the number three firm in your market, wouldn't it be a tragedy to end as the number five firm after the recovery because you focused on surviving and other firms focused on how they could reposition themselves to take more of the market? This issue applies equally to individual brokers as it does to their firms.

THE FIRST STEP

In our coaching business we know the first thing a business must understand is where it is in the cycle of building and growing a business. Our framework for this is called Stages™. It looks like a typically hockey stick model from business school. However, the biggest difference is that we focus on the feelings that are predominant at any particular point in the business cycle and the impact those feelings have on:

- The communication in the business
- The focus of the business
- The decision making
- The energy or lack of it that occurs at each stage

The framework looks like that shown in Figure 9.4.

The normal conversation around Stages would be looking at several contexts such as:

- Where is the market on Stages?
- Where are your clients on Stages?

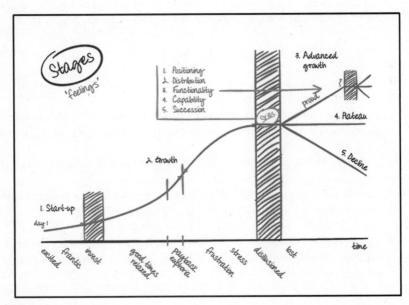

FIGURE 9.4 Stages Framework
Source: Shirlaws™

- Where is your staff on Stages?
- Where are you on Stages in your career?

What business cycle discussions do businesses need to focus on when designing their recovery strategy?

In the Start-Up Stage, the feelings at the beginning of the business go from excited to frantic and then to anxious as the business bumps up against the learning around what it will need to do to really be in business with the stress that is created as initial funding starts to run out. At some point the business runs into the large first Brick Wall labeled "invest." The business either figures out what is needed to invest in to get the business to really work well or it fails at this point.

In the later part of the cycle, the business experiences frustration and stress as it learns how to grow the capacity of the business to handle the growth. The frustration and stress typically turn to disillusionment as the business struggles to adapt to the new structures and practices that are required to run a larger business. Many people languish or pine for the "good old days" as they continue to find that *the structures and strategies they used in the early years of the business simply don't adapt to a larger business.*

What is it that is causing this stress that eventually leads to disillusion? After years of study we have found there are five key things a business must be able to do successfully in order to get through this Second Brick Wall (the later part of the Growth Stage) and into Advanced Growth. They are:

- Positioning: Do you have a clear position in the mind of your clients/market?
- Distribution: Do you have a robust lead sourcing through multiple channels to feed your business?
- Functionality: Do you have a clear process for running the business that supports productivity, revenue production, and long-term strategy and profit?
- Capability: Have you built a plan around what capabilities you will need to develop to grow the business to the next stage?
- Succession: Have you built out a plan that supports your internal staff and your external relationships to grow with your business?

If a business gets these five areas correct, the path to advanced growth is shorter and much more enjoyable. If a business does not address these areas, *it can be stuck in a circular series of restructures* that eventually lead to the decline of the business.

When the market shifts this dramatically, as it has recently, many businesses are thrown into dealing with these five key areas without any awareness of what to do about them.

TAKING ADVANTAGE OF THE RECOVERY—FIND THE OPPORTUNITY GAPS

These are the gaps that appear as the market pulls back and restructures. In order to find these gaps, you need to know where to look. We have found that markets shrink the same way that they have grown. It is similar to reverse engineering.

We have seen that businesses fundamentally grow in six ways:

- Positioning—Repositioning to stand out in a market.
- Distribution—Changing the way or number of channels by which prospects come to the business.
- New products—Adding some new relevant service lines.
- Leverage—Growing the business by adding head count, growing territories, or mergers and acquisitions.
- Pricing and packaging—Are products or services bundled or unbundled and how are they priced?
- Client base management—Is the quality of your clients upgraded by attracting more profitable or more strategic clients?

The Opportunities

If we distill this down to the opportunity gaps for brokers and brokerage companies, it could look like this:

- Positioning—What positions will open up as a result of the pull back or failure of other brokerage companies? Which key owners and tenants will be open to new relationships?
- Distribution—What new market channels (sources of new prospects) can you build that will be supported, feeding your business a higher quality and volume of prospects?
- New products—With the shift in ownership and competitors, what new or additional service lines will make you more relevant to the clients you seek to attract?
- Leverage—What new geographic markets could you shift into by attracting key brokers, brokerage partners, or acquiring a firm or a team?
- Bundling/Integration—What new ways of bundling or integrating service lines would be more appealing to your clients and give you a competitive advantage?
- Client base management—Are you getting the highly profitable clients in the market or are you playing with a lower tier of client that takes the same amount of time and cost to work with but is much less profitable? Can you upgrade the type of clients you want to work with by letting go of

some of your unprofitable, non-strategic clients and focusing the extra capacity on making your strongest clients into raving referral sources?

The key choices here are to:

- Pick one or more of these six areas.
- Develop a complete strategy to drive success in that area. These must include:
  - A vision of the key outcomes you expect.
  - What blueprint or strategy you will use to get you there.
  - What key resources and specific plans you will need to implement your strategy?

What cultural and commercial fears or push back will you need to address with other brokers, clients, or vendors?

- Complete the design of your strategy early so that you start looking for the business, partners, alliances, skills, resources, and relationships you will need to make this successful.
- Create at least a two-phase strategy—early and late recovery.
  - Early recovery will address the early shift in ownerships that are likely to occur in 2010 and 2011.
  - Later recovery strategies will be about how you will leverage your early recovery strategy to maximize your position and market share.

It will be important to address the early versus late recovery—just off the bottom versus mid recovery of values and their impact on relationships and positioning.

Some straight talk about driving strategy in your business:

The reality is that building strategy is a skill that is developed and/or hired into a firm or practice. Those that build this strategy capability into their business will have the means to survive this current downturn, and, most important, they will be able to substantially reposition themselves and create a more promising and profitable trajectory for their business.

After working with thousands of firms, we have found a straightforward approach to effectively driving strategy in a business:

1. Pick three projects (and no more than three) that you will focus on designing and implementing in your business.
2. Don't start a fourth project until all three are completed.

When managing these projects, make sure each project is clearly outlined with a vision, strategy, and implementation plan. We outline these as:

- Vision—*Why* we are doing this—the outcomes and impact.
- Strategy—*What* we are going to do—the plan or blueprint.
- Implementation—*How* we are going to complete the project—the tools, resources, time lines, etc.

In our work with sales organizations and brokerage firms, we have found that a large number of brokers and firms don't get a clear vision, skip the blueprint or planning stage, and launch into the details. The lack of a clear plan leads to breakdowns and missed expectations. To be successful in maximizing the opportunity that this real estate tsunami offers, a complete strategy will be essential to winning.

SUMMARY

The key to facing the recession successfully is to understand that this is just another cycle. We will always have cycles. As businesspeople, we have a choice: hunker down to ride it out and see what happens or:

1. Learn to navigate the cycle.
2. Determine what skills will be important in each part of the cycle.
3. Build those skills into the business before they are needed so that you can catch the first wave of the cycle when resources are cheap and the market makes its biggest moves.

Our goal is to remind you that you have a choice as to which road you choose in dealing with this recession and the resulting fallout in the real estate community. We hope you will take the road that leads to opportunity.

CHAPTER 10

How to Ride a Tsunami with Expertise

Interview with Former Banker Turned Prolific Commercial Broker, Anton Qiu

As the commercial real estate market slowly stalled in 2009, I was fortunate to have an associate with whom I could collaborate in the area of bank's special assets and REO disposition. Anton Qiu and I have collaborated on numerous projects since I started with TRI Commercial in 2000. In 2009 we worked together on the evaluation and disposition of foreclosed office buildings and residential condo developments. Anton is a Principal of TRI Commercial Real Estate Services, Inc. CORFAC International, one of the largest full-service commercial real estate firms in northern California. His clientele includes banks, insurance companies, publicly traded REITs, and domestic and foreign wealth investors. Anton is a former investment banker himself. He has distinguished himself by achieving the high honor of being the number 1 company-wide top producer for an unprecedented eight consecutive years (2002–2009) (I won in 2001!), as well as the recipient of many industry awards. Anton has handled more than $1 billion of commercial real estate transactions. His resume includes Board Member and Treasurer of San Francisco-Shanghai Sister City Committee for nearly 20 years; he has travelled extensively in Asia and China and previously served on the Board of Directors of The Pacific Bank, a NASDAQ listed company. He is also a past Chairman of the Asian Council of the San Francisco Association of Realtors, a board member of Chinese-American Real Estate Association and a Past President of the China Business Association that he co-founded.

Anton graciously agreed to share his knowledge and expertise as a commercial broker and former bank executive for this book. His interview provides additional depth on the commercial real estate debt issue and its impact on the commercial real estate market, lenders, investors, and brokers.

Here you will gain further insight to the commercial real estate tsunami from someone who rides that wave with mastery every day.

Tony Wood: What is your theory about how the commercial real estate industry as a whole got into this mess with over-inflated values and over-leveraged property nationwide, even world-wide?

Anton Qiu: My "theory" is that this whole mess is mainly due to two reasons. First, the Fed and Alan Greenspan kept interest rates way too low for too long after the dotcom meltdown, which created huge liquidity (lending) that eventually fueled more and more speculative investments in real estate. I distinctively remember during the 1999–2001 dotcom craze, many new companies with a short history and no revenues still able to go IPO, and stock prices would rocket overnight with valuations in hundreds of "potential" multiples. Half the people in our office (and many of my friends in other professions such as legal, accounting etc.) were all busy buying stocks on the Internet (remember the "day trader" phenomenon?) and talking about how much paper profit was made over lunch. Taxi drivers and restaurant wait staffs were always asking for "stock tips" or better yet, had a "hot one" for me every time I got into a taxi or a restaurant. We all know what happened when that bubble burst: Every single person that I know lost money. People were so scared of the stock market, they sold everything and moved the money to CDs and money-market funds (sound familiar?), but when the interest rate stayed at such a low level for such a long period of time, the yield wasn't there. Thus, everyone was looking for a better place to invest, and real estate became the choice or sometimes the only option for many.

The second reason is that Wall Street got involved. Every time WS gets involved in some industry, everything becomes big, bigger than you would ever imagine! I did my first couple of CMBS loans in the mid to late 1990s. The investment banking unit that handles these loans was small and usually staffed with very seasoned real estate executives or commercial loan underwriters. The rates were a little more attractive, but the underwriting was tough and the borrowers had to jump through lots of "hoops" to get a deal done. The CMBS loans typically offered 10-year fixed rate with 30-year amortization (the typical comparable bank deals will only offer five- to seven-year fixed at higher rates and only 20- to 25-year amortization and lower LTV), however, many investors would rather deal with the bank to avoid the lengthy process and significantly more paperwork required by these CMBS loans. Then sometime in 2003–2004, I started getting aggressive calls from people who were not traditional lenders (banks and insurance companies) quoting great rates and attractive terms on all types of commercial loans. The exception was construction loans (part of the reason why a lot of regional banks got involved with so many construction loans is because they couldn't compete with the CMBS loan's pricing and terms). As the CMBS rates kept going down, the pools got bigger, amortization got longer (some deals had 40-year terms), and with commercial real estate prices going up and cap rates going down, we began to see IO (interest only) loans so the deal could meet the DSCR (debt service coverage ratio). Then the underwriting got sloppy. All of sudden, instead of seasoned underwriters and loan brokers, it was marketing people or "business development officers." One good example was that one of my clients sold an apartment property with $6,000,000 in proceeds for a 1031 exchange; we looked at a shopping center, which was offered at $20,000,000. I took the deal to several traditional lenders and on average the quotes were in 6.75 to 7.25 percent range with 65 to 70 percent LTV (with good credit and balance sheet) and 20- to 25-year amortization. Then, I took it to Merrill Lynch, Deutsche Bank, and several other CMBS lenders. The most aggressive quote we got was 80 percent LTV, with first four years IO, then six-year based on 90 bspt over 10-year Treasury (at the time was about 4.7 percent so the all-in rate would be about 5.6 percent fixed), and 35-year amortization, non-recourse (this is big, as most banks would require personal guarantee). It became so attractive, my client's exact words to me were "Anton, this is a no brainer, I can do this deal and buy another shopping center so I can leverage and own $30,000,000 worth of shopping centers instead of just one $20,000,000." As all those investment bankers made millions in profit, appetites grew for such products from investors all over the world. The rating agencies were sleeping at the switch and more exotic products such as CMBS insurance, re-insurance, and derivatives all became a part of the cycle to generate more capital to be put in work in this sector and on and on it went

Last, as part of the consequences of the first reason, while the Fed let liquidity loose and fueled the CMBS securitization market, it and the rest of the government oversight agencies didn't see the potential problems and therefore didn't institute proper regulations letting this whole CMBS derivative market get more and more out of hand.

TW: How have you seen these conditions affect your investment clients in the United States versus your investment clients from other parts of the world?
AQ: I have not done a "normal" investment deal since Q4 of 2008. Most investors are sitting on their hands, keeping the cash, not willing to do anything as they see the market will go down further in the coming years. Other investors are having significant problems in either cash flow or refinancing and face losing their properties. Many of my institutional and overseas clients are now talking about investments buying distressed assets from lenders.

There is extremely high interest from Asia, particularly China, to invest in U.S. real estate and other segments.

TW: What kind of conversations are you having with your long-term investment clients these days? Those who purchased during this last "boom" in commercial real estate values?
AQ: Mostly when the phone rings, there is a problem that needs my opinion or assistance. We are talking about restructuring loans, losing tenants, and banks are not lending.

TW: What are the owners most concerned with and what are the few investors in the market looking for now versus two years ago?
AQ: Owners are mostly concerned about losing tenants, reducing rent to keep some tenants and banks putting pressure on higher vacancies, DSCR violations, etc. New investors are mostly looking for distressed assets, huge discounts, and not pulling the trigger.

TW: How are you able to assist them with these concerns?
AQ: We are constantly assisting clients in renegotiation of leases, providing timely market information to validate certain decisions, and even accompanying clients to their lenders to assist in restructuring loans. We are also advising a lot of clients in structuring "blend and extend" deals (i.e., if a good tenant has two to four years left on a lease at a rental rate substantially higher than current market rates), where we would recommend approaching the tenants to offer reducing their rates for the next couple of years in exchange for the tenant's making a commitment to extend the lease for two to three years firm at a slightly lower rate. It is usually a win-win situation—while the landlord loses some revenue for now, it helps the tenant in this difficult economy. The landlord gains longer-term stability with a good tenant and can have a more "bankable" lease to show the lender.

TW: How has this market affected you professionally and personally?
AQ: I find myself more energetic in a difficult and challenging market. The fact that so many of my clients and lenders need my professional advice is the reason why I choose to be in this profession. Luckily, due to a number of institutional and bank clients that I have worked with over the years, my production didn't suffer much. I do find myself working even longer hours now with a busier schedule because there is no such thing as a "no brainer" deal anymore. Everything I am working on has problems or complex issues. The change of the economy and market didn't impact me personally much; however, everyone is aware of the situation. We find ourselves in the same shoes as many other families talking about saving and not spending unnecessarily. Probably the toughest thing is constantly hearing that friends and

family members lost their jobs. A couple of parents in my kid's school recently lost jobs and might not be able to afford the tuition next year. That puts everything in perspective.

TW: I know many commercial real estate brokers are spending more time searching the Internet for jobs and updating their resumes than showing, selling, or leasing properties these days. How have you managed not only to just survive in this market but actually thrive, staying number one in our company for yet another year?

AQ: The fact that our profession exists is because commercial real estate is an imperfect market (compared to residential). I remember when I closed one of my last big 1031 exchange deals, which involved multiple transactions, in August 2008, then suddenly the market seemed to have stopped. I had six live transactions at various stages, including some that I would almost consider a "done deal" during the normal time, all fell apart during the fourth quarter of last year, mainly because of the financing (either pulled or couldn't get what was expected). I thought hard and long during the holidays and realized that I had to reformulate my business plan. I began calling all of my bank contacts that I had established over the years, taking many to lunches and setting a lot of meetings. Not surprisingly, every bank had begun to see some problem assets or initial loan delinquencies. I offered my professional valuation services to many banks, charged them nothing, and gave them my fast turnaround (an appraisal report usually takes four to eight weeks). Also, we usually have the most up-to-date comparables and statistics. These reports turn out to be very helpful to banks when they deal with regulators and auditors. Many of these relationships lead to transactions when the bank forecloses on these properties or decides to sell the notes. Close to 75 percent of my revenue this year came from helping lenders sell distressed notes and REOs.

TW: That is something we have in common. What have you done to adapt your services offered to meet the market's new demands?

AQ: Because of my background as a former investment banker and analyst, and as a former research director when I first came into this commercial real estate business, I've always taken an analytic and professional approach to the business. I try to separate myself by providing a high level of service and the ability to provide professional advice and opinions. I am always willing to go the extra mile for a client. I've continued to do the same, but just with a slightly different focus, more on lenders, opportunity funds, and distressed asset buyers.

TW: What are you recommending to your clients who find themselves over-leveraged in their properties?

AQ: Try to retain tenants even it means reducing rent in the near term. Vacancy and re-leasing costs can eventually kill a shopping center or other investment property. Approach the lender and be honest with it, try to work out a loan restructuring deal, but be realistic. Most lenders usually prefer workouts versus taking the property back.

TW: Let's talk a bit about how we as brokers help them navigate getting a loan workout, short sale, or deed in lieu started?

AQ: We assist them to be fully prepared before approaching the lender for a workout. We get comps, market data, and as much relevant information together as possible and present them in a professional way. As a former director of a publicly traded bank, I sat on every bank committee, including loan committees, for four+ years. I know that most bankers like customers who are well prepared (not sloppy) and will be more sympathetic and reasonable if someone is honest and straightforward.

TW: At some point we have to recommend they give up, right?

AQ: Yes. When the asset is so far upside down and the borrower has absolutely no additional resources (or it is a non-recourse loan).

TW: Do you agree with me that commercial loan modifications will become as common as residential loan mods?

AQ: Yes, the new FDIC rule changes will also direct more banks to renegotiation and restructuring of loans. However, I still expect a huge number of them are not going to work since the assets are so far upside down.

TW: What are the biggest differences/considerations between residential and commercial loan mods?

AQ: Commercial real estate has less of a "human" face compared to residential real estate. Every house is directly occupied by a family, kids, parents, grandparents, dogs, cats . . . that's more of a "human" story, while most commercial real estate is for investment, those who are typically portrayed as "rich people." It gets less public sympathy.

TW: We represent lenders on their special assets and REOs. How are they adapting to this challenging environment?

AQ: Their process is matched with your first chart, going from super aggressive, optimism, to deny, wondering, then realizing that it is just going to be "fact of life."

TW: Capitulation in some cases if they wait too long. Do you see some of the lenders really working the system to postpone or otherwise delay the inevitable by "extend and pretend" methodologies?

AQ: Absolutely. Many are still using last year's appraisal reports as the base. One bank's asset manager, when I told her that the 20-plus offers that

I generated on a loan sale indicated that at the best, the market value was about 50 cents on the dollar, her response was, "Then we will just use that old appraisal to stall the auditors for another couple of quarters."

TW: What are the typical lender's approaches when dealing with REOs these days?
AQ: Typically, if it is an REO, the value has already been written down and the charge off already took place and was reported so the lender wants to move fast and get rid of it since an REO ties up the capital.

TW: How do you deal with your broker valuations being so different from the appraisals the lenders throw back at you when there is a disparity?
AQ: I usually tell the banks that appraisers always call us to get updated comps (usually a month or two after the sale is closed or published or even longer). My professional opinion and updated comps would give them more accurate information and market statics. Luckily, I had to go head on with some appraisers over the course of the time, and often have better supporting data, so many of my lender clients are now asking me to help review the new appraisals to see if there are any issues (usually I find either they are using very old comps since there are no sales in the same areas, or using wrong operating data, etc.).

TW: Do you agree that lenders beginning to see that appraisals are based on history, and brokers have the freedom to valuate from the present and better evaluate future trends?
AQ: Yes.

TW: Please explain how the lenders are allowed to do this under applicable bank regulations?
AQ: Many bank auditors actually understand this. I have also been an expert witness in some cases, and being a former bank loan committee chair, I know that broker opinions are valuable.

Several of my bank clients have now adopted the practice of asking brokers to submit a BOR (broker opinion report), and they often use that as a benchmark to decide whether they want to sell the note or foreclose on them.

TW: I know when we work together, in our transactions representing lenders on their special assets and REOs, we find lenders have different approaches depending on their company's policies as well as more broad regulatory rules. What are the most common ways lenders go about resolving their special assets issues and disposition of their REOs and the differences and rationale between them?

AQ: I think that there is less of the "rule of the thumb" and more of the special case by case. Smaller assets are usually done with typical standards that Special Asset and REO departments set. A large asset that could impact earnings or capital will be dealt with very differently by each bank depending upon whether it is publicly traded, privately held, how strong the capital ratio is, and so on. It also depends on asset class and product types. For example, most lenders would prefer (or I will advise them) not to foreclose and take back broken, unfinished condo projects because the lender might immediately take on a 10-year liability that is not desirable at all, since it didn't build the project.

TW: In regards to your international investment clientele, how have the current commercial market challenges affected their investment criteria?
AQ: Most of my overseas clients are eager to look at the opportunities and desire to make some sort of investment in U.S. real estate in the next few years.

TW: What are they indicating are their biggest concerns and objectives when considering a new investment property?
AQ: Location, property type, management issues, and professional know-how post investment.

You need to be more sophisticated. Not only have the product knowledge but speak institutional language. You must be able to provide exceptional service and add value to their approach while also being able to deliver the product.

TW: As you look at the commercial real estate markets for 2010, what areas or property types are you most concerned about and what changes (regulatory or otherwise) do you see will be helpful to the situation?
AQ: Retail will probably be the biggest problem area, followed by office, then industrial types. There will be no construction for several years; multi-family is on top of the wish list for most investors.

CHAPTER 11

A Life Preserver for Your Family

Therapeutic Strategies for Family Survival in a Tough Economy—Donna Wood, MA, MFT

Whether you're a commercial real estate agent, a loan broker, a developer, or business owner, the pressure to earn an adequate living in this tumultuous financial environment is more palpable by the day. Fortunes have been lost, from modest to significant, including everything from real estate to jobs to material possessions. Turning to a colleague or industry friend for support, emotional or financial, may result in little more than a reminder to count your blessings. It's challenging to move forward, with a positive attitude, and do the things necessary for survival when you're surrounded by such devastation.

People are struggling to survive in this economy and the commercial real estate industry has been hit hard, the residential crash intensifying the impact. Many, already confronted with the decline in home values, or struggling with a foreclosure or short sale, now face a situation in which income is dramatically reduced or, for some, nonexistent. That's an incredible amount of stress for anyone to manage. Not surprisingly, and reflective of the overall economy, the rate of anxiety and depression in the United States is increasing.

From *FamilyBroke: Therapeutic RX and simple strategies for Family Survival in a Tough Economy*, a book by Donna Wood to be released in 2010. Donna Wood, a psychotherapist and writer practicing "Whole Person Psychotherapy," provides E-Therapy through her website and individual, group and family therapy from her practice, in Northern California. Donna is available for public speaking engagements and consultation as well. Contact Donna through her website: www.familybroke.com or donna@donnawoodmft.com.

It's critical, now more than ever, to rely on those closest to you for support and, likewise, to make sure they are getting the support they need as well. Family and friends can be the life preserver needed to stay afloat in this commercial real estate tsunami. Unfortunately, oftentimes, when things are difficult at work and finances are tight, family dynamics end up contributing to the stress rather than reducing it, creating a downward spiral that is difficult to overcome. Home should be a refuge; a safe place to unwind, nourish ourselves and recharge. Likewise, friendships shouldn't be an additional source of stress. If your personal life is as challenging as your professional life, it's time for some simple changes that could have considerable impact on the bottom line. Outlined below are several steps you can take to begin the process of creating a more balanced home life and bringing your family together through tough times.

OPEN THE LINES OF COMMUNICATION

A common reaction to financial and job-related difficulty is to isolate oneself, turning inward, rather than reaching out, working harder and more diligently to remediate the situation. And in this case, it's a situation that may not change any time soon. Thwarted efforts can quickly lead to feelings of hopelessness and despair. Your family and friends know when you feel anxious, depressed, or tense. Because it's not spoken doesn't mean it's not heard. Negative emotions reveal themselves in everything we do. Unless you acknowledge the stress you are under and communicate your feelings effectively, these negative emotions may be misinterpreted by those closest to you. The result is distance and isolation rather than closeness and support. When such an imbalance occurs, anxiety and depression, health issues, and marital problems are not uncommon. Your personal struggle to overcome the current real estate tsunami, if handled in isolation, may threaten your safe harbor of home.

Make concerted efforts to discuss feelings with your spouse, family, and friends in a relaxed environment. Set a few ground rules for these discussions: no interruptions, no blaming statements, reflect back what the other has said. The goal here is to allow everyone to express him- or herself and feel heard in a safe, nonthreatening environment. Work on resolving issues at another time as it tends to take us from a place of feeling to a place of thinking. It's important to connect on an emotional level with those closest to you, as it will strengthen the base from which you work. When we feel understood and loved for who we are, despite our struggles, we are empowered and better able to deal with whatever comes our way. As the commercial real estate industry continues to be hit hard, it's going to take a lot of strong, grounded, resilient individuals to turn things around. You've got to start at home, making sure you've got a rock-solid base to stand on, strong enough to withstand the impact of the coming tsunami.

WORK AS A TEAM

Take a look at your family dynamics and fundamental beliefs about family hierarchy. Are you trying to maintain a position of control within your family? If so, try shifting to a more neutral position. Frequently, even if unspoken, the primary income generator will view him- or herself as head of household, or the only person in control. This creates difficulty in several ways. First, if you are in control and things are not going well, the burden is upon you and you alone to fix the problem. This can be incredibly isolating and stressful. Second, the family becomes part of that burden, as you strive to take care of them in a difficult economy. Negative feelings can emerge on both sides, even in the most loving relationships. Third, anxiety tends to increase when loved ones are not clear about the situation at hand and consulted regarding possible solutions. The unspoken message is that you are the only one capable of solving problems. Finally, if acting in isolation, for whatever reason, you will not be able to fully depend on your family for much-needed support, because they are not being included as part of the process. At a time when creative and strategic solutions are necessary, both at work and within the home, it is essential that families work together and support each other in the struggle for financial stability.

Shifting the way you view family and self within the family is a good start. If family is viewed as a team, and you are a part of the team, then the burden shifts to the whole. You no longer need to carry all that weight alone. No team can be fully effective if all the players are not working together. Functioning as a team player does not mean that you are not an authority, a mother, a father, or a leader. It means that you view all family members as important contributors to the success of the whole. Define the roles and responsibilities of your family team together, taking care to include your children in a manner that is developmentally appropriate. Create a plan with your family team for reducing expenses and gaining financial stability. Meet regularly to discuss progress, difficulties, and successes. Be sure to allow time for gratitude and praise regarding everyone's accomplishments, including your own. It's important that all members of a family team be acknowledged for their efforts, even if it doesn't materialize into financial remuneration.

This is an opportunity to shift from a position of carrying a burden to being part of a supportive team that works together in troubled times.

People, even little ones, want to help. It is a fundamental human need to make a contribution in the world and, for many, that begins in the home. When a family operates as a team, all members have an opportunity to contribute to the whole. Conflict and negative emotions will be reduced as family members feel a sense of inclusion, responsibility, and increased control of their destiny. You will likely feel supported and enjoy sharing the responsibility of financial success with your family.

BE TRUTHFUL ABOUT FINANCES

Be honest with your family team about finances. Financial hardship creates a feeling of insecurity for everyone in the family, not just the income earners. Honesty will allow for development of a realistic budget, with input from all, greatly influencing the level of buy-in and commitment. The kids will know when you're cutting back. Failing to acknowledge your financial situation will not protect them, but rather will create confusion and insecurity because what they experience and what they are told are not congruent. Being honest and factual, in a developmentally appropriate manner, will provide the kids a sense of safety, because they won't need to make up their own scary stories about what could be going on. Give them the opportunity to ask questions, discuss feelings, and work through negative emotions together in a healthy manner. A new level of closeness can emerge as you work together toward financial success. In addition, when things go awry, no one will feel misled, but rather a part of a team that has lost for the moment.

Admitting financial difficulty doesn't mean admitting failure. Tough times come and go, just like times of prosperity. As hard as it is live through, this economic crisis is a grounding, humbling experience that will serve as a reminder that no one is financially invincible. Your kids will benefit from knowing that difficult times exist and learning how to confront problems in a positive, interrelated manner rather than in fear and isolation. Remember that you are not alone. Many people are struggling financially, forced to do things they never thought they would have to do to make ends meet. This is a reflection of the economy, not a person's worth.

SHIFT YOUR PERSPECTIVE

Acknowledge the upside of down. Look at the opportunities living with hardship provides. Try reframing how you view a situation, from negative to positive. This simple strategy can have a surprisingly positive impact on your mood. For example, cancelling the family vacation, while disappointing, could afford more time for family interaction with less stress. No packing, no planning, less expense. Likewise, home improvement projects, while previously relegated to a contractor, could be an opportunity to work closely with your son or daughter, building that shed together or painting the living room or replacing a sink. You'll feel more pride of ownership in your home and a greater sense of accomplishment as you personally conquer the problem. You will also enjoy the camaraderie of working together with your family members. Begin to look at a lack of money as an opportunity for closeness, creativity, and small successes. The key here is to take a proactive stance, making choices that will have a dual benefit of saving money and creating closeness, for example, and promoting it as such within the family.

In addition to changing perspective regarding particular situations, altering how you view your life, letting go of what was, is important. Redefine "normal" in the face of financial distress. Maybe it was normal to take a couple of vacations a year. Maybe it was "normal" to enroll the kids in private school or to have a personal coach or to have a maid or two cars (or three or four!). Maybe it was normal to live in a 5,000 sq ft house in an apparently affluent neighborhood. I say "apparent" as the affluence was likely based on a strong economy. Let go of the whole idea of "normal" in relation to money and define life in terms of your values and beliefs, a much more stable and consistent guide. When I ask clients about their original goals and desires in life, rarely is it reflected in what they have built up materially. Try to get back to basics about who you are and what kind of person you wanted to be. Are you on the path you once chose? Recommit to that path or, if necessary, change it.

Most of us don't need a lot of money to live a happy, fulfilling life. This economy is helping families get back to the basics. Living within means feels good and reduces stress as the baggage of debt falls away. As the economy shifts in a more positive direction, everyone can benefit from the lessons learned and lifestyle changes made during this tough economic time. The economy will ebb and flow and go through cycles. A family needs to be able to adapt to the changes, learning to live with financial struggle, operating from a stable base that will come together in crisis rather than be torn apart. If a family is only able to function well in good times, the pressure to perform will be even greater on the income generators. Making a fundamental shift in family perspective, from expectation to thankfulness, will help everyone feel a sense appreciation for his or her efforts, at home and in the workplace.

Defining wants from needs and prioritizing is another important step in shifting your perspective and an effective way to reduce arguments and tame resentment before it gets out of control. If you are in financial distress, a family rule for the time being may be that wants are put on the back burner; a wish list for better economic times. While initially frustrating, this approach will help everyone to manage expectations and create an internal strategy for dealing with the situation at hand. If one knows that the year ahead will be tough, expectations can be altered and feelings acknowledged, rather than a more reactive approach of denying requests and allowing frustrations to build.

OPEN YOURSELF TO THE IDEA OF CHANGE

Sometimes our best efforts will not be enough to achieve success. In this situation, one can move forward, continuing to do the same, frustrated with the outcome, or do something different. As simplistic as this may sound, when faced with crisis, many people cling to what they know out of fear. While this may be the most comfortable approach, to do the same, but with more effort or more intensity or more of it, it is not necessarily the best approach. This can increase stress and anxiety as effort does not equate to success. Your family may feel anxious as well if they see and feel your frustration and are powerless to help. A family decision needs to be made regarding how much you are willing to risk by continuing to do the same. If you allow yourself to step out of the confines of "what was" and really investigate "what could be," you may be able to come up with a plan that works better for the whole family. Perhaps it's time to change professions, or make a shift within your profession, looking carefully at all your skills and the current needs in the marketplace. Perhaps it's time to work part-time, freeing up your spouse's time to work. Would relocating help? Can you earn additional income at home? Could you go back to school? Could the whole family get involved in a family business that still allows you to work, but provides an alternative income source? What is possible? Strategizing with your spouse and, when things are more concrete, with the whole family team, will allow everyone to feel involved and respected and take the full burden off of you. Again, coming together as a team, rather than approaching this as an individual will result in creative, sometimes brilliant, solutions that your family will embrace and could lead you out of financial distress. At the very least, you will have the support of your family. While the thought of making such change may be frightening, and requires courage, imagine staying on the same path with little or no improvement. Would that be more frightening? Change can be a good thing and, quite often, a much-needed change doesn't happen until we are in crisis. Being proactive and creative will help to reduce reactivity and feelings of helplessness.

DEFINE SUCCESS IN THE CONTEXT OF LIFE

This step is essential in creating balance within your life. Your life is about a lot more than how much money you bring in. Parent, husband, wife, daughter, son, friend, community member, parishioner, mentor, volunteer are some of the many roles you may have, each requiring effort and each bringing certain returns to you. While you may be struggling financially, how are you doing on the parent front? When was the last time you tried to surprise your spouse with a loving gesture? How involved are you in your community? Financial success only pays the bills; it doesn't create the life you live. It can enhance it. It can shape it. But it doesn't create it. It doesn't change how your daughter looks at you or how your spouse feels about you or how many true friends you have. Remind yourself constantly of who you are and the successes that you do have, both personally and professionally. If you don't know who you are, find out. If you don't like who you are, create change. This is an opportunity to reshape your life rather than allowing life to shape you by default. You have the power and ability to make positive life changes, regardless of the economy, and you have the right to celebrate and revel in your successes, even if they are not of a financial nature.

NURTURE THE WHOLE PERSON

Whatever you do, regardless of the choices you make, optimal success will be difficult if your body and brain are not functioning properly. Stress further complicates matters as an increase in cortisol, the stress hormone, can cause weight gain, fatigue, lack of mental clarity, and insomnia and has been linked to depression and anxiety. One of the best ways to counteract stress and elevate mood is to eat healthy foods and exercise regularly. Get back to basics with your body. Exercise daily, even if it's only for half an hour. Studies clearly indicate that moderate exercise has numerous health and psychological benefits. In fact, combined with psychotherapy, research shows that exercise can be more effective than medication in combating depression and anxiety and reducing stress. Furthermore, prescription drugs may not be an option if your healthcare coverage has been terminated. Exercising is free and effective and a great way to connect with your family. Try hiking, biking, or walking around your neighborhood together. You'll feel closer to your loved ones and a more vibrant part of the community, both of which will make you feel better. Exercise can help increase self-esteem as well, which may be waning as you struggle to survive in this economy. You can set realistic goals in your exercise routine and attain them, creating a sense of mastery over something in your life. In addition, the health benefits will help to generate feelings of well-being and initiate positive momentum. Always check with your health care provider before commencing a new physically challenging routine.

Try these guidelines for reducing the stress in your life and bringing your personal life back into balance. Seek professional help regarding depression, anxiety, or any psychological issues that interfere with adequate daily functioning. A qualified psychologist or psychotherapist will be able to provide an assessment and make appropriate recommendations. Look for a practitioner who considers the whole person, as your mental health is closely tied to your environment and physical well-being. If you're not certain whether it's time to contact a professional, consider the following indicators: sleeping more or less than usual, feeling hopeless, repetitive unproductive and negative thoughts, irritability, difficulty focusing and staying on task, increase in alcohol or drug use, highly emotional reactions, excessive worry or fear, change in self-care or appetite, and lethargy. These are some key indicators that additional help may be warranted.

FLOTATION DEVICES

In the wake of this worldwide financial crisis, mental health services and government programs are springing up everywhere in an effort to assist people in managing the emotional and financial impact. The Internet is an easy and efficient way to tap into these resources. Obtain a referral, research conditions, complete online assessments, research available government aid or find a support group without leaving your home. A well-respected nonprofit organization offering mental health screening and assistance, a crisis hotline, resources, information, prescription assistance referrals, and insurance advocacy and more is Mental Health America (www.mentalhealthamerica.net). One of its programs is "Live Your Life Well" (www.liveyourlifewell.org), a website related to managing stress and living a healthier, more balanced life. It's easy to use and comprehensive. The President's networkofcare.org is a new website designed to streamline the process of finding government assistance. You can research various government resources and assistance programs and find support all in one place. Many therapists are also offering E-Therapy, psychotherapy via e-mail or Skype. While E-Therapy can't replace in-person psychotherapy, it can be effective in working through a particular problem or situation and is a quick and easy way to begin the psychotherapy process without leaving home. A new site dedicated to providing psychotherapeutic consultation, support, and information specific to those in the commercial real estate industry is www.familybroke.com.

CORPORATE ASSISTANCE

Don't forget to turn to your employer for assistance through Employee Assistance Programs (EAPs) and various other company-funded programs designed to support employees struggling with various life stressors. EAP programs are confidential and usually free. If you are an independent contractor, check your private insurance policy for mental health coverage and assistance. Management, at the very least, should keep in mind that employees are people with fundamental human needs. Just like family members, employees need to feel a part of the process. They need information about the current situation, communication from above, recognition for efforts, morale-boosting activities, freedom and encouragement to grow as individuals and to feel a part of team.

Employers seeking to better support their employees during this difficult time could benefit from a workplace productivity consultant. Humannatureatwork.com is a great resource focused on improving employee productivity by managing based on the principles of human nature. You'll find, among many other topics, comprehensive information regarding workplace stress, how to identify it, the associated cost, and how to reduce it. The founder has written several articles and books that savvy companies will want to read. If your company isn't actively supporting your efforts in this difficult market, pass on some information to management, including this book.

Conclusion

From Despondency to Optimism

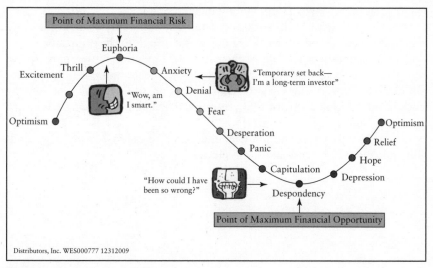

FIGURE C.1 The Cycle of Market Emotions

Source: Westcore Funds distributed by ALPS. Copyright September 1998, Denver Investments, all rights reserved.

This book predicts a historic event that will impact the world of commercial real estate, a tsunami wave of commercial real estate debt maturities, foreclosures and loss in value the likes of which have not been seen before. The resulting damages are yet to be fully determined. An appropriate ending to this book may be to simply say, "Stay tuned and stay alert." The final result of the conditions outlined and chronicled herein will be revealed over the coming months and years ahead. Heeding the advice and guidance of the contributors in this book will surely benefit anyone navigating the turbulent waters we see ahead and help limit their damages.

As we move through the phases of this wave, many will observe first-hand the casualty count in terms of commercial real estate values, foreclosures, and the widespread impact it will cause. In the short run there is no question; fortunes will be lost, hundreds of banks closed, and thousands of careers re-determined, but in the long run the resulting healthier conditions will ultimately show this market's cycle of correction was necessary. There will be lessons learned and rules created for a new paradigm of commercial real estate investment, ownership, and financing.

I anticipate with hard work and determination many of us in the commercial real estate industry will see our way through to the other side. Some will survive simply as a result of their fortunate position in the marketplace during this time, while others will succeed with their acquired skills to reposition themselves as quickly and accurately as possible. It will take tenacity and daring to look forward and create anew instead of looking backward for reassurance.

To ride out this economic tsunami, accurate tactical knowledge skillfully applied will be critical to our success.

Resources

Accountants

Michael Hawes
Michael Hawes & Associates
4168 Douglas Blvd, Suite 300
Granite Bay, CA 95746
Phone: (916) 791-9095
Fax: (916) 791-9098

John Whitfield
Moss Adams
Phone: (530) 748-0524
E-mail: john.whitfield@mossadams.com

Appraisers

David M. Rosenthal
President and CEO
Curtis-Rosenthal, Inc.
5959 W. Century Blvd., Suite 1010
Los Angeles, CA 90045
Phone: (310) 215-0482
Fax: (310) 215-3089
E-mail: drosenthal@curtisrosenthal.com

Paul Stansky
PO BOX 8231
Citrus Heights, CA 95621
Phone: (916) 780-9365
Fax: (916) 780-9423
E-mail: pstanskysr@comcast.net

Asset Disposition Advisors

Edward D. Durnil, CEO

Tranzon Asset Advisors

1108-A North Dixie Ave.

Elizabethtown, KY 42701

Phone: (270) 769-0284

Fax: (270) 737-7695

Cell: (502) 741-1331

E-mail: edurnil@tranzon.com

Business Coaching and Consultants

Bill Duthler

SCORE

Business Consulting

Phone: (916) 303-3273

E-mail: dbduthler@pacbell.net

Toosje Koll

Resources-US

Phone: (916) 787-8405

E-mail: toosje.koll@resources-us.com

Lois Lang

Evolve Partner Group

Management Consulting and Succession Planning

Phone: (209) 608-5465

E-mail: Lois.lang@evolvepartnergroup.com

Eric Palmaer, CEO

Vistage International, Inc.

5603 Carlile Court

Granite Bay, CA 95746

Phone: (916) 797-1837

Fax: (916) 797-4026

E-mail: eric.palmaer@vistage.com

Website: www.vistage.com

Curt Rocca
DCA Capital Partners
Investment Fund/Mergers & Acquisitions Consulting
Phone: (916) 960-5353
E-mail: crocca@dcapartners.com

Rebecca Young
Shirlaws Global Business Coaching
560 S. Winchester Blvd.
San Jose, CA 95128
Phone: (925) 683-3215
E-mail: ryoung@shirlawscoaching.com
Website: www.shirlawscoaching.com

Capital Markets Consultants

Michael Singh
Managing Director
Jones Lang LaSalle Americas
2049 Century Park East, Suite 2750
Los Angeles, CA 90067
Phone: (310) 595-3801

Capital Sources

Guy K. Johnson
President/CEO
Johnson Capital
2603 Main St., Suite 200
Irvine, CA 92614
Phone: (949) 660-1999
Fax: (949) 660-1998
E-mail: guyjohnson@johnsoncapital.com

Barry Simson
Partner
SM Realty Advisors
3232 Cross Creek Rd.
Malibu, CA 90265
Phone: (310) 457-9441
Fax: (310) 457-9442
E-mail: re.financier@verizon.net

Barry Hacker
Managing Director (Real Estate Investment Banker)
Navigant Capital
One California Plaza
300 South Grand, 29th Floor
Los Angeles, CA 90071
Phone: (213) 670-2734
Fax: (213) 670-3250
E-mail: barry.hacker@navigantcapitaladvisors.com

Corporate Financing

David Gruebele
Second Angel Bancorp
Phone: (408) 398-8475
E-mail: dg@secondangel.net

CRE Brokerage Services and Consulting

Tony Wood, Sr.
Vice President
TRI Commercial Real Estate Services
Phone: (916) 390-1274
E-mail: tony@tonywoodconsulting.com
Website: www.tonywoodconsulting.com

CRE Consultants

Cynthia Nelson (Financial and CRE Consultants)
FTI Consulting
633 W. Fifth Street, 16th Floor
Los Angeles, CA 90071
Phone: (213) 452-6026
Fax: (213) 452-6098
E-mail: cynthia.nelson@fticonsulting.com

Larry Schiff
Senior Manager—Financial Risk Management
KPMG LLP
355 South Grand Avenue, Suite 2000
Los Angeles, CA 90071
Phone: (213) 955-8497
Fax: (213) 652-0759
E-mail: lschiff@kpmg.com

Jane F. Hoffner
Financial and CRE Advisor—Deal Structuring
Managing Director
The Bascom Group
26 Corporate Park Drive, Suite 200
Irvine, CA 92606
Phone: (949) 955-0888 x30
Fax: (949) 955-0188
E-mail: jhoffner@bascomgroup.com

Stephen G. Torres, P.G.
Apex Companies, LLC
531 West Golf Road
Arlington Heights, IL 60005
Phone: (847) 956-8589 x204
Mobile: (312) 215-0109
Fax: (847) 956-8619
E-mail: storres@apexcos.com
Website: www.apexcos.com

Michael A. Schwartz, Esq. (CRE Consultant)
Managing Director, Real Estate Group
RSM McGladrey, Inc.
One South Wacker Drive, Suite 800
Chicago, IL 60606
Phone: (312) 634-3062
Fax: (312) 634-3027
E-mail: michael.schwartz@rsmi.com

Georgia Perkey (CRE Business & Tech Consultants)
Managing Partner
iNPOINT Advisors
Phone: (310) 732-6448
E-mail: gperkey@inpointadvisors.com

Economists

Sam Chandan, PhD, FRICS
President & Chief Economist
Real Estate Econometrics
1120 Avenue of the Americas, 4th Floor
New York, NY 10036
Phone: (212) 626-6600
Fax: (212) 626-6730
E-mail: chandan@reeconometrics.com

Nancy D. Sidhu
Senior Economist
444 South Flower St., 34th Floor
Los Angeles, CA 90071
Phone: (213) 622-4300
Fax: (213) 622-7100
E-mail: nancy.sidhu@laedc.org

Christopher Thornberg, PhD
Founding Principal
Beacon Economics
12100 Wilshire Boulevard, Suite 1040
Los Angeles, CA 90025
Phone: (310) 472-3274
E-mail: Chris@BeaconEcon.com

Employee and Customer Loyalty Expert

Larry Hill
CalPro Research
Phone: (916) 435-9196
E-mail: lhill@calproresearch.com

Environmental

Joseph P. Derhake
President
Partner Engineering and Science
2101 Rosecrans Avenue, Suite 4270
El Segundo, CA 90245
Fax: (310) 615-4544
E-mail: joe@partneresi.com

Brian Devine, Senior Vice President
GaiaTech—Atlanta
3343 Peachtree Road NE, Ste. M20A
Atlanta, GA 30326
Phone: (404) 812-0001 x224
E-mail: bdevine@gaiatech.com

Jim Robert
Senior Geologist
Trihydro Corporation
2710 169th Street, S.E.
Bothell, WA 98012
Phone: (425) 485-0414
Fax: (815) 846-8445
E-mail: jrobert@trihydro.com

Daniel W. Petersen, PhD, P.G.
Environmental Resources Management, Inc.
704 North Deerpath Drive
Vernon Hills, IL 60061
Phone: (847) 932-1300
Mobile: (847) 830-1422
Fax: (847) 258-8501
E-mail: dan.petersen@erm.com
Website: www.erm.com

Hotel Accommodations

Micael Jeffries
Springhill Suites by Marriott
10593 Fairway Drive
Roseville, CA 95678
Phone: (916) 782-2989
E-mail: rosevilleSHS@pharaldson.com

Hotel Consultants

Alan X. Reay
President
Atlas Hospitality Group
2500 Michelson Drive, Suite 110
Irvine, CA 92612
Phone: (949) 622-3409
Fax: (949) 622-3410
E-mail: alan@atlashospitality.com

John L. Strauss
Executive Vice President
Jones Lang LaSalle
515 South Flower Street, Suite 1300
Los Angeles, CA 90071
Phone: (213) 239-6360
Fax: (213) 239-6100
E-mail: john.strauss@am.jll.com

Human Resource Outsourcing

Karen O'Hara
HR TO GO
Human Resource Outsourcing
Phone: (916) 444-6200
E-mail: KarenOhara@hrtogo.com

Information

GlobeSt.com
Incisive Media
120 Broadway, Floor 5
New York, NY 10271
John Salustri, Editorial Director
Phone: (212) 457-9400
Fax: (646) 822-5358

California Real Estate Journal
915 East First Street
Los Angeles, CA 90012
Michael Gottlieb, Editor
Phone: (213) 229-5308
E-mail: Michael_Gottlieb@dailyjournal.com

GreenPearl.com
Brian Klebash, Director of Events
36 East 23rd Street
New York, NY 10010
Phone: (646) 862-9391

Moody's Investors Services
99 Church Street
8th Floor
New York, NY 10007
Phone: (212) 553-1653

Commercial REO Brokers Association (CREOBA)
George Aguel, Membership Coordinator
2629 Townsgate Road, Suite 250
Westlake Village, CA 91361
Phone: (818) 483-1597 x111
E-mail: george.aguel@creoba.com

Insurance: General and Property Risk

Mark Carlin
Producer
Lockton Insurance Brokers, Inc.
725 S. Figueroa St., 35th Floor
Los Angeles, CA 90017-5524
Phone: (213) 689-0507
Fax: (213) 689-0521
E-mail: mcarlin@Lockton.com

Rose Nordbrock
Senior Vice President
Venbrook Insurance Services
6320 Canoga Avenue, 12th Floor
Woodland Hills, CA 91367
Phone: (818) 598-8900
Fax: (818) 598-8910
E-mail: Venbrook@mail.vresp.com

Philip Schaaphok
Farmers Insurance
P. O. Box 859
341 Tres Pinos Rd. # 205B
Hollister, CA 95023-5589
Phone: (831) 634-4420
Fax: (831) 634-4422

Marshann Varley
Client Executive
Marsh Risk & Insurance Brokers
777 Figueroa St., 23rd Floor
Los Angeles, CA 90017
Phone: (213) 346-5597
E-mail: marshann.varley@marsh.com

Dave Ward
Interwest Insurance
Phone: (916) 488-3100
E-mail: dward@iwins.com

IT Outsoucing

John Pyron
IBNS Inc
Phone: (916) 381-4267
E-mail: jpyron@ibns-inc.com

Lawyers

Jeb Burton (Estate)
The Burton Law Firm
555 University Ave, Ste. 275
Sacramento, CA 95825
Phone: (916) 570-2740
Fax: (916) 570-2744
E-mail: jburton@lawburton.com

Chris Chediak
Partner, Corporate Law
Weintraub Genshlea Chediak
400 Capitol Mall
Sacramento, CA 95814
Sacramento, CA
Phone: (916) 558-6016
E-mail: chediak@weintraub.com

Brian Coggins (Bankrupcy)
Coggins Johnston, LLP
2281 Lava Ridge Court, Suite 320
Roseville, CA 95661
Phone: (916) 780-4253
E-mail: BCoggins@cjmlawyers.com

Maura B. O'Connor
Partner
Seyfarth Shaw LLP (National full service law firm doing real estate transactions, financings, workouts, and foreclosures)
333 South Hope Street, Suite 3900
Los Angeles, CA 90071-1406
Phone: (213) 270-9631
Fax: (213) 270-9601
E-mail: moconnor@seyfarth.com
Website: www.seyfarth.com

Glenn Peterson (Business Litigation)
Millstone, Peterson & Watts, LLP
2267 Lava Ridge Ct.
Roseville, CA 95661
Phone: (916) 780-8222
Fax: (916) 780-8775
E-mail: gpeterson@mpwlaw.net

Charles Trainor (Real Estate)
Trainor Fairbrook
980 Fulton Ave.
Sacramento, CA 95825
Phone: (916) 929-7000
Fax: (916) 929-7111
E-mail: ctrainor@trainorfairbrook.com

Lender—Credit Union

Dawn Cooper
Vice President—Commercial Real Estate
Business Partners LLC
9301 Winnetka Ave
Chatsworth, CA 91311
Phone: (818) 836-6364
Toll-free: (800) 894-8328
E-mail: dawn.cooper@businesspartnersllc.com

Lender—National

Ashil Abhat
SVP, Business Banking Market Executive
Global Commercial Banking
Bank of America Merrill Lynch
Bank of America, N.A.
Phone: (916) 878-3112
Cell: (916) 765-3617
E-mail: ashil.abhat@bankofamerica.com

Lenders—Private

Paul B. Elis
President
PMB Capital, Inc.
4606 Park Mirasol
Calabasas, CA 91302
Phone: (818) 222-1035
Fax: (818) 222-1036
E-mail: paulelis@pmbcapital.com

Rich Strock
Strock Realty and Financial
4962 El Camino Real
Suite #104
Los Altos, CA 94022
Phone: (650) 938-1955
Fax: (650) 644-0446
E-mail: strock1@aol.com

Richard Clayton Temme
President
R.C. Temme Corporation
21777 Ventura Blvd., Suite 211
Woodland Hills, CA 91364
Phone: (818) 999-2274
Fax: (818) 703-0126
E-mail: rich@rctemme.com

Lender—SBA Loans

Brian Kerfoot
CDC Small Business Finance
1545 River Park Drive #203
Sacramento, CA 95815
Phone: (916) 565-8102
Fax: (916) 925-5593
E-mail: bkerfoot@cdcloans.com

Mortgage Brokers

L. Scott Clark
Pacific Southwest Realty Services
11911 San Vicente Blvd., Suite 390
Los Angeles, CA 90049
Phone: (310) 440-2301
E-mail: sclark@psrs.com

Public Relations and Marketing

Ann Bouchard
Principal
Matrix Manager/Bouchard Marketing
1430 Blue Oaks Blvd., Suite 290
Roseville, CA 95747
Phone: (916) 783-6161
E-mail: ann@bouchardcommunications.com
Website: www.bouchardmarketing.com

Kohn Communications
419 N. Larchmont Blvd. #332
Los Angeles, CA 90004
Phone: (310) 652-1442
E-mail: larry@kohncommunications.com
Website: www.kohncommunications.com

Mayo Communications
7248 Bernadine Ave., Suite #2
West Hills, CA 91307
George S. McQuade, III, Vice President, New Business/Media Relations
Phone: (818) 340-5300
Fax: (818) 340-2550
E-mail: george@mayocommunications.com

Mickelson & Associates, Inc.
8957 Hanna Avenue
West Hills, CA 91304
Anastasia Mickelson, President
Phone: (818) 384-3670
E-mail: anastasia@mickelsonassociates.com

MWW Group, Inc.
660 South Figueroa Street, Suite 1400
Los Angeles, CA 90017
Coby King, Senior Vice President and General Manager
Fax: (213) 486-6501
E-mail: cking@mww.com

John Segale
Precision Public Relations
Phone: (916) 960-5341
E-mail: jsegale@precisionpublicrelations.com

Receivers

Judy Hoffman
Senior Vice President
Trigild
12707 High Bluff Drive
Suite 300
San Diego, CA 92130
Phone: (858) 720-6720
Fax: (858) 720-6705
E-mail: judy.hoffman@trigild.com

Gregory T. Rickard
Equassure, Inc.
2041 Rosecrans Avenue, Suite 354
El Segundo, CA 90245
Phone: (310) 335-9343
Fax: (310) 469-0118
E-mail: grickard@equassure.com

David P. Stapleton
President
Stapleton Group
515 South Flower Street, Suite 3600
Los Angeles, CA 9007
Phone: (213) 236-3597
Fax: (213) 236-3501
E-mail: david.stapleton@gmail.com

Mark J. Weinstein
President
MJW Investments
1640 5th Street, Suite 112
Santa Monica, CA 90401
Phone: (310) 395-3430 x217
Fax: (310) 395-3145
E-mail: mweinstein@mjwinvestments.com

Bellann Raile
Receiver
Cordes & Company
2102 Business Center Drive #130
Irvine, CA 92612
Phone: (949) 433-7435
Fax: (949) 253-4105
E-mail: Bellann@cordesco.com

Recruiting/Video Networking

Mark Sadovnick
President and Managing Partner
Sadovnick Partners/Rez Buzz
11680 Duque Dr., Suite 250
Studio City, CA 91604
Phone: (323) 654-2469
E-mail: mark@corpshorts.com
Website: www.rezbuzz.com

Retained Executive Search Firms

Dave Sanders
Worldbridge Partners
Phone: (916) 960-5362
E-mail: dave@worldbridgepartners.com

Surveyors

Lonny Sheek
Psomas & Associates
3187 Red Hill Ave., Suite 250
Costa Mesa, CA 92626
Phone: (714) 751-7373
Fax: (714) 545-8883

Timothy Blair
Surveyors Group, Inc.
9001 Foothills Blvd, Suite 150
Roseville, CA 95747
Phone: (916) 789-0822
Fax: (916) 789-0824
E-mail: surveyorsgroup@surewest.net

The Mollenhauer Group
411 West Fifth St., Fourth Floor
Los Angeles, CA 90013
Bob Mollenhauer
Richard Snedaker
Phone: (213) 624-2661
Fax: (213) 614-1863

Title Insurance

Selina I. Parelskin
Senior Vice President
Major Accounts—National Commercial and Non-Judicial Foreclosure
Specialization
Fidelity National Title
915 Wilshire Blvd.
Suite 2125
Los Angeles, CA 90017
Phone: (213) 452-7111
Fax: (213) 683-9921
E-mail: sparelskin@fnf.com

Sharon Yarber
Vice President, Senior Commercial Underwriting Counsel
Commonwealth/LandAmerica Title Insurance Company
915 Wilshire Blvd., Suite 2100
Los Angeles, CA 90013
Phone: (213) 330-3035
Fax: (213) 330-3120
E-mail: syarber@landam.com

James D. Prendergast
Senior Vice President General Counsel
The First American Corporation
Phone: (800) 700-1191
Fax: (714) 250-8694
E-mail: jprendergast@firstam.com

Val Berlin Douglass
Senior Account Manager
North American Title Company
Northern California Region
Phone: (916) 782-1241
Fax: (916) 677-1689
E-mail: valthetitlegal@yahoo.com

Jeffrey Schick
Vice President
First American Title Insurance Company
118 South Beverly Drive, Suite 222
Beverly Hills, CA 90212
Phone: (310) 925-9080
Fax: (310) 273-1857
E-mail: jschick@firstam.com

Trustee Services

Beacon Default Management, Inc.
15260 Ventura Boulevard, Suite 1150
Sherman Oaks, CA 91403
Selina I. Parelskin, President
Veronique Collin, Director of Sales
Phone: (818) 501-9800
Fax: (818) 501-9801
E-mail: parelskins@beacondefault.com
E-mail: collinv@beacondefault.com

Melinda Zabroski-Theilen
Senior Account Executive
Old Republic Title
1000 Burnett Avenue, Suite 400
Concord, CA 94520
Phone: (925) 687-7880
Fax: (925) 798-3283
E-mail: MelindaT@ortc.com

Wealth Management

Jim McCarthy
Legacy Capital Inc
Phone: (916) 783-6200
E-mail: Jim@legacycapitalinc.com

About the Author

Tony Wood is an award-winning veteran of the commercial real estate industry. With more than 30 years' experience and a consistent track record as a top producer, he has successfully worked with all types of commercial property with a wide range of client profiles. Tony's resume includes the valuation, leasing, sales, and management of office, retail, industrial, and residential income investment properties, and single tenant, triple net leased investments throughout the Western United States. He has been retained as a consultant to law and accounting firms and also represents lending institutions in the evaluation and disposition of their Special Assets and Commercial REOs.

Along with his extensive commercial real estate brokerage experience, Tony Wood has been an active leader in the commercial real estate industry and is an invited guest speaker and contributor to numerous media outlets.

For more information, visit the author's website: www.tonywoodconsulting.com.

Contributors

Matthew Anderson, Partner
Foresight Analytics LLC
1633 Broadway, Suite B
Oakland, CA 94612
Phone: (510) 893-1760
Cell: (510) 393-7405
E-mail: m.anderson@foresightanalytics.com

CCIM Institute
430 N. Michigan Ave, Suite 800
Chicago, IL 60611
Phone: (800) 621-7027
Website: www.ccim.com

CoStar Group Inc.
2 Bethesda Metro Center
10th Floor
Bethesda, MD 20814-5388
Phone: (800) 204-5960 or (301) 215-8300
Website: www.costar.com

Dr. Sam Chandan, Chief Economist
Real Estate Econometrics
1120 Avenue of the Americas, 4th Floor
New York, NY 10036
Phone: (212) 626-6600
E-mail: support@reeconometrics.com
Website: www.reeconometrics.com

Tom Loeswick and Rebecca Young
Shirlaws Business Coaching
560 S. Winchester Blvd.
San Jose, CA 95128
Phone: (925) 683-3215
E-mail: ryoung@shirlawscoaching.com
Website: www.shirlawscoaching.com or www.shirlawsonline.com

Charles A. McClure, CCIM, CRE, FRICS
P.O. Box 802047
Dallas, TX 75380-2047
Phone: (972) 663-3738 Office
E-mail: mmcclure@mcclureusa.com

Maura O'Connor, Partner
Seyfarth Shaw LLP
333 South Hope Street
Suite 3900
Los Angeles, CA 90071-1406
Phone: (213) 270-9631
E-mail: moconnor@seyfarth.com

Cynthia Shelton, CCIM, CRE
Colliers Arnold Commercial Real Estate
The Milano-Shelton Retail Team
Providing Retail Investment Sales Solutions in Florida
Phone: (407) 362-6142
E-mail: cshelton@colliersarnold.com

Eric Von Berg, CMB, Principal
Newmark Realty Capital, Inc.
595 Market Street, Suite 2700
San Francisco, Ca 94105
Phone: (415) 956-9922 Direct
E-mail: evonberg@e-newmark.com

Donna Wood, MA, MFT
Phone: (916) 878-6332
E-mail: donnawoodmft@familybroke.com
Website: www.familybroke.com or www.donnawoodmft.com

Tony Wood
Tony Wood Consulting
Sr. Vice President
TRI Commercial-CORFAC International
DRE Lic. 00549071
Phone: (916) 390-1274
E-mail: tony@tonywoodconsulting.com
Website: www.tonywoodconsulting.com

Index

Buyers (*Continued*)
cash is king, 145–146
due diligence, importance of,
146–148
in the tsunami marketplace, 143–145

CALPers, 9
Cap rates, 12, 22, 128, 165
Capital markets consultants, 183
Cash flow, 138
Cash is king, 145–146
CCIM Institute, 8–9, 14
Certified Commercial Investment
Member (CCIM), 8–9
Chandan, Sam, 79–89
Client base management, 159–160
Client service, 154
Code violations, 147
Collateral, 62, 63, 64, 72, 74, 75, 76,
77, 111–115, 118, 129, 136
Colliers Arnold, 20, 200
Colliers Parrish, 150
Commercial broker price opinions, 97
Commercial debt maturities, xvi, 12,
28, 102
Commercial lending institutions, 93
Commercial loan maturities, 6
Commercial loan modifications,
97–100
Commercial mortgage backed securities
(CMBS), 4–5, 10–11, 62, 63–64,
74–75, 79–81, 101, 109,
126–127, 134, 164–165
AAA-rated, 62
current conditions in, 74–75
issuance, 61
loans, 164–165
super duper Treasury spread, 64
"Commercial Mortgage Outlook:
Growing Pains in Mortgage
Maturities" (2009 report), 5
Commercial mortgage portfolios, 79,
80, 81, 83, 85
"Commercial Property Faces Crisis"
(*Wall Street Journal*), 4, 5
Commercial real estate (CRE)

brokerage services and consulting,
184
crisis, 76, 163–170
current conditions in, 74–75
consultants, 184–186
debt maturities, 61
required equity for, 66
debt outstanding, 60
Federal Reserve activities to help
revitalize markets, 75
Federal Reserve supervisory activities
related to, 75–76
foreclosures, xvi–xvii, 5, 28, 131,
industry, xi, xv–xvi, 8, 9, 14, 17–18,
20–21, 24, 27, 55, 56, 59, 68,
69, 97, 104, 107, 125, 131, 133,
164, 171, 172, 178
mortgage markets and policy
interventions, 79–80
sales volume, 71
sector, 57
"Commercial Real Estate Will
Collapse" (*Intelligent
Investing*), 6
Comps, 11, 128, 168, 169
Condition of property, 115
Congress, xvii, 12, 14, 56, 97, 106, 107
Construction defects, 147
Construction and land loan defaults
(2009), 89
Consumer spending, 58, 59, 70
Core courses, 14–15
Cornell, Christopher, 5
CoStar Group, 27–29
CoStar Realty Information, Inc., major
metro market data surveys,
29–53
Arizona: Phoenix region, 30–31
comparison report for, 30
vacancy and rental rates, 31
California: Los Angeles–Orange
County region, 32–33
comparison report for, 32
vacancy and rental rates, 33
California: Sacramento region, 34–35
comparison report for, 34

Term Asset-Backed Loan Facility
    (TALF), 62–64, 72, 75, 77
Three monkeys, 93
Tishman Speyer, 81–83
Title insurance, 195–196
Tony Wood Consulting, 124
Toxic assets, 64, 98
Trainor, Tim, 27
Tranches, 75, 105, 126
Treasury Regulations, Subchapter A,
    Section 1.860G-2(b)(3)(i), 80
TRI commercial, 163
Triple net, 13, 22
Trustee services, 196

UCC, 115, 118, 139
Unemployment rate, 14

Vacancy rates, 12, 19, 70, 74, 87, 121,
    151. *See also* CoStar Realty
    Information, Inc., major metro
    market data surveys
Valuation, 4, 28, 64, 66, 73, 77, 97–99,
    123, 128, 164, 167, 169
Von Berg, Eric, 100–110

Wall Street Journal, 28
Walter, Paul, 5
Westcore, 143
Wharton School, University of
    Pennsylvania, 79
Wood, Donna, 171–179

Workouts, commercial loan, 110–119,
    123–125
  from the borrower's perspective,
    135–141
    borrower leverage, 135
    borrower mindset, 135
    cash flow considerations, 138
    common ground, finding,
      136–137
    considering all options, 141
    insurance coverages, 140
    intrinsic value of the property, 138
    knowing the property, 137
    maintenance and waste, 139–140
    personal or pass-through liability,
      other areas of, 140
    reviewing the loan documents,
      139, 141
    what not to do, 137
  from the lender's perspective,
    110–119
    business review, 116
    conclusion and caveat, 119
    documenting and closing the
      workout, 118
    early stage moves, lender's,
      116–117
    legal review, 114–115
    lender leverage, 112–114
    lender mindset, 111–112
    long lead items, 118–119
    negotiating the workout, 117–118